London Walks
in easy English

Patrick Gubbins

Published by Sigma Leisure – an imprint of
Sigma Press, Stobart House, Pontyclerc, Penybanc Road
Ammanford, Carmarthenshire SA18 3HP

British Library Cataloguing in Publication Data

A CIP record for this book is available from the British Library

ISBN: 978-1-85058-932-7

Typesetting and Design by: Sigma Press, Ammanford, Carms

Maps: © Bute Cartographics

Photographs: © Patrick Gubbins

Cover photograph: © main photograph: The Houses of Parliament looking south-west from the South Bank, with Westminster Bridge in the foreground.
left to right: Exotic cuisines on offer at the Sunday Upmarket in Brick Lane; A peaceful Sunday horse-ride in Hyde Park; The famous Sherlock Holmes pub and museum near Trafalgar Square

Printed by: Akcent Media Ltd

Contents

Introduction

Welcome to London!

Whether you live here or you're just visiting, I want you to enjoy yourself in this city and get to know it better than the other 8 million people you're sharing it with.

How is this book different from other books of self-guided walks? In several ways:

Firstly, it's written in "easy English". Most books of self-guided walks are written for people who speak English as a first language, so are too difficult for people who don't. To understand the walks in this book, your English only needs to be conversational-level. We use no difficult words or complicated grammar. When we have to use a word you may not know, we explain its meaning. But "easy English" doesn't mean the text in this book is childish, and we hope you'll enjoy it even if English is your first language.

The second way this book is different is that most other books of self-guided walks do one walk per area; but why should you be especially interested in "Clerkenwell" or "Marylebone"? Instead, we do one walk per theme, meaning that you can choose walks on topics that interest you, such as "River London" or "Royal London".

The third difference is that this book is actually interesting. Most books of walks take you into an ordinary-looking street and tell you that someone died there 500 years ago. In this book we'll do better.

We'll go to lively and colourful places with atmosphere, where you can see real Londoners doing what they do every day. In the "Shopping London" walks, for example, we take you right into shops and recommend exotic but cheap food you can taste. In "Legal London" we take you inside courtrooms where you can see real trials happening. In "Clever London" we take you inside the buildings of the University of London, and even into lectures (lessons) if they're happening. You'll see London at its busy and exciting best. We'll do some history when it's interesting, but we won't only do history – unlike some books. You'll see the famous sights but you'll also see a lot of things that very few people know about.

I had a lot of adventures while collecting material for this book. I got covered in paint; I nearly fell in a canal; I was stopped and security-checked by the police; when I didn't know if a building was private, I just went in – sometimes with no problems, but many times I was seen and told to get out immediately.

But it was all fun, and I want to hear about the fun you have while on these walks. Contact me via www.patrickgubbins.com, where you'll also find links to the web sites mentioned in this book, plus one or two extra walks for you to enjoy.

To walk in a city is the best way to get to know it. But you already know that – it's why you picked up this book.

Patrick Gubbins
London, 2012

Royal London

Start and end:	Westminster tube station
Length:	3 miles (5 kilometres)
Time taken:	1 hour plus shopping time
Eat and drink:	There are lots of restaurants near Victoria Station and several options within St James's Park
Includes:	Whitehall, Banqueting House, Horse Guards, The Mall, Marlborough House, St James's Palace, Spencer House (family home of Diana, Princess of Wales), Lancaster House, Clarence House (home of Prince Charles and the Duchess of Cornwall), Buckingham Palace, Royal Mews (where royal cars, carriages and horses are kept), Goring Hotel, Guards Museum, Westminster Abbey
Best time:	Any, though if you want to visit the museums the opening times are: Banqueting House, Monday to Saturday 10 am - 5 pm; Household Cavalry Museum, daily 10 am - 5 pm; Royal Mews, open irregularly - Google "royal mews London"; the State Rooms of Buckingham Palace are open during the summer every year - Google "visit Buckingham Palace"; Guards Museum, daily 10 am - 4 pm; Westminster Abbey, Monday to Saturday 9.30 am - 3.30 pm except religious holidays - call 020 7222 5152

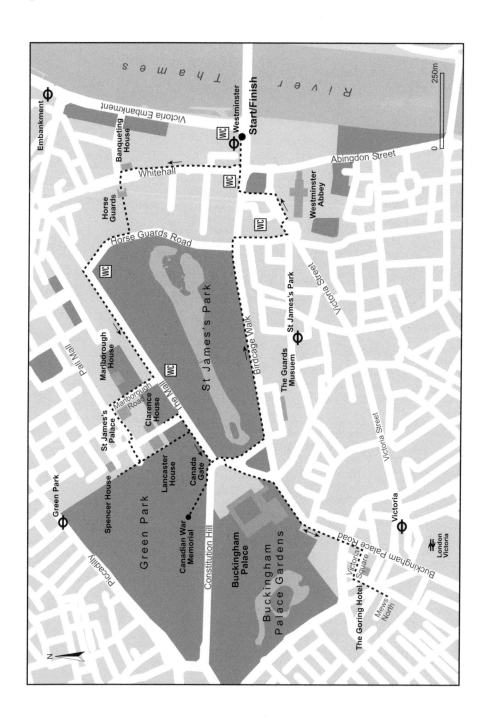

Introduction

The British monarchy is the most famous in the world, and its traditions, costumes and parades together form one of the main attractions that brings foreign visitors to Britain.

Historically the monarchies of many other European countries refused to give up political power and were destroyed; Britain's monarchy gave up political power and survived. Today it has found several new functions: ceremonial, diplomatic and charitable, for example. It has a more modern image nowadays, especially the youngest generation. But there is still something "royal" about the British monarchy; it is still "posh" and still has an feeling of "mystique".

Foreign visitors to London often do not realise that the monarchy is unpopular with some British people, who say it is unnecessary, expensive, old-fashioned or that it represents an unhealthy class system. The monarchy's supporters like the glamour and the continuity of tradition, or simply find the royal personalities and their lifestyles interesting. Love it or hate it, the monarchy is certainly a frequent topic of conversation and attracts constant interest from the media.

This walk takes you to locations in London which have been important in the lives of today's royal family but also in the lives of kings and queens in hundreds of years of British history. We include famous sights like Buckingham Palace as well as many other interesting places that are little known to tourists and locals.

Walk

Whitehall

Leave Westminster Station, walk west to Whitehall and stand looking north. This street is named after the Palace of Whitehall, built here in 1530 and used by Henry VIII and later monarchs as a residence and government administration centre.

As we all know, one wife was not enough for Henry, and neither was just one palace. He almost emptied England's

Looking north up Whitehall

bank account by building or improving more than 50 palaces during his lifetime, although to be fair to him, he did obtain some of them at no cost by the brilliantly simple method of confiscating them. The greatest and grandest palace of all was the one he built here: The Palace of Whitehall, which had over 1500 rooms and was the biggest royal palace in Europe, with its own tennis court, bowling green and sports fields. Sadly, it was not to last. In January 1698 a washerwoman who was heating water let her fire get out of control, and within a few hours Henry's palace was a smoking ruin. Only one part of it survived, as we will see.

300 years later Whitehall is still the centre of government in Britain, and is home to many government buildings including the Department of Work and Pensions, the Department of Health, and the Ministry of Defence, all on your right as you walk north. Because of the large number of government buildings in this street, the British often use the word "Whitehall" to mean the government bureaucracy in general.

Walk north to Banqueting House on your right, on the corner of Whitehall and Horse Guards Avenue.

Banqueting House

Banqueting House is the only significant part of the original Palace of Whitehall that has survived to today. It has a marvellous ceiling painting by Peter Paul Rubens, and

The Banqueting House on Whitehall

Horse Guards

Horse Guards, with soldiers of the Household Cavalry on guard outside

the underground crypt still exists. The house is open for visits on most days.

If you meet a member of today's Royal Family, there is one event that took place at the Banqueting House which you should perhaps not mention: the execution of King Charles I in 1649. After Charles' army lost the English Civil War he was brought to the Banqueting House to meet his fate. It was a cold January day and Charles wore two shirts, not to avoid catching cold but to prevent any winter shivers, which to the watching crowds might have suggested fear.

Looking at the front of the Banqueting House you will see that three of the first-floor windows have small balconies. It was from the middle window that Charles stepped out onto a specially-built wooden platform and shook hands with his executioner. He made a short speech to the crowds and then was beheaded with one stroke of a sword.

His execution came as a great shock to the English, who until that moment had seen the monarch as a representative of God on Earth. Charles' death temporarily ended royal rule in Britain; 11 years of civilian government followed, until the monarchy was restored in 1660 and Charles' son became king.

Nowadays royal transitions are much more peaceful; although you might argue that the quick and painless death Charles received was kinder than the long-term agony that today's monarchy suffers from the international press.

Cross Whitehall to Horse Guards.

Horse Guards is a large white Palladian building constructed in 1753; it was the headquarters of the British Army until 1904. Outside it two soldiers of the Household Cavalry usually stand guard (or rather sit, on horseback) for many hours at a time. Unofficially, no tourist's visit to England is complete until he has been photographed beside them.

The Household Cavalry Museum, on the north side of the building, tells the story of the regiment.

Guards changing ceremony at Horse Guards Parade

Walk west into the building's yard and continue through the arches into Horse Guards Parade, a large open area that has been the scene of military parades and royal celebrations since the time of Henry VIII. Polo championships have been held in Horse Guards Parade, and it is the location of the 2012 Olympic volleyball competition.

Walk to the centre of Horse Guards Parade and look back towards the arch you have just walked through. On the clock above, the figure "2" has a black background, supposedly referring to the time of day that Charles I was executed.

Look to the south side of Horse Guards. Behind the brick wall is the garden of 10 Downing St, where the Prime Minister lives. Following a bomb attack on the house in 1991, visitors are no longer allowed near the wall.

Cross to the west side of Horse Guards Parade, then walk north up Horse Guards Road to the long straight red-coloured road called The Mall, which leads from Trafalgar Square to Buckingham Palace.

The Mall

The Mall, looking west towards Buckingham Palace

The Mall was created by architect Aston Webb in the early twentieth century as a ceremonial road like those of other capital cities such as Berlin, Paris and Washington DC.

According to an urban myth, if there is ever a foreign invasion of London The Mall will be used as a runway for the Royal Family and the government to escape by plane (although in the centre of the road are traffic lights which will need to be removed first). There are also stories of a secret train station under Buckingham Palace which joins the Piccadilly Line, which the Royal Family could use in an emergency to reach Heathrow Airport and fly from there to Canada.

Cross to the north side of The Mall and walk west in the direction of Buckingham Palace. On your right are the Institute of Contemporary Art (open Wednesday to Sunday, midday till late, often with free exhibitions), the Duke of York Column, the Royal Society, and the Royal College of Pathologists.

Just before Marlborough Road on your right the brick frontage of Marlborough House can be seen in its large garden.

Marlborough House

Marlborough House, with flags of Commonwealth countries flying in the garden

Marlborough House has many royal associations. It was designed by architect Christopher Wren in 1711 for Sarah Churchill, the Duchess of Marlborough, who was a close friend of Queen Anne and an ancestor of both Winston Churchill and Diana, Princess of Wales. Later it was the home of Edward VII before he became king in 1901, and was the centre of London high society. From 1936 it was the home of the widow of King George V. When Elizabeth became queen in 1953 she donated the building to the Commonwealth Secretariat, the parliament of the British Commonwealth. This explains the number of flags around the edge of the building's garden.

The interior of Marlborough House is magnificent, and impressive paintings cover many of the walls. Unfortunately the building is open to visitors only for Open House weekend every September.

Turn right into Marlborough Road and continue north until you see St James's Palace on your left and the yellow facade of Queen's Chapel on your right.

St James's Palace

St James's Palace, home of several members of the Royal Family

St James's Palace was built by – you guessed it – Henry VIII in 1536. It became the monarchy's official residence after Whitehall Palace was destroyed by fire, and many monarchs have slept here including Charles I on the night before his execution - if he slept. Today it is the administrative centre of the monarchy and the London home of Princess Anne and the two daughters of Sarah Ferguson, Princesses Beatrice and Alexandra.

Because St James's Palace was the official royal residence for 300 years, foreign ambassadors in London are still called "Ambassador to the Court of St James" rather than "Ambassador to the United Kingdom".

St James's is a working palace so it is closed to the public. The only exception to that rule is the Queen's Chapel, which is open for Sunday services at 8.30 and 11.30 between Easter and July.

St James' Palace used to cover what is now Marlborough Rd until 1809 when a fire destroyed some buildings. The buildings were never rebuilt, and instead a road was laid on the site, which is why the chapel is today separate from the palace.

Walk north to the end of Marlborough Road, then walk west along Pall Mall into Cleveland Row and continue to a square where on your left you will see policemen guarding the lane to Prince Charles' home, Clarence House, of which there are better views later in the walk. Go to the north-west corner of the square and walk west along a narrow lane to Green Park. Turn north, and you will see on your right first one large mansion house in white stone, and then a second, Spencer House.

Spencer House

Spencer House, ancestral London home of Princess Diana's family

Spencer House is owned by the aristocratic Spencer family, which included Princess Diana, who before she married Prince Charles was Lady Diana Spencer. The house was previously the family's London residence. The Spencers' main ancestral home is Althorp in Northamptonshire, about 60 miles north of London, but the family built Spencer House in 1756 in order to be near the monarch.

The house was formerly the scene of numerous high society parties held by successive Spencer generations but has not been lived in by a Spencer for many years. The family rents it to a private company.

You can hire the house, but a better way to become part of Diana's family history, and for perhaps a thousandth of the cost, is to simply take a guided tour, which is possible any Sunday except during January and August.

Now walk south back to The Mall, turn left and walk east. Immediately on your left is Lancaster House.

Lancaster House

View towards Lancaster House

Lancaster House was built in 1825 by the Duke of York and Albany, and has beautiful Louis XIV-style interiors and a superb staircase. When Queen Victoria visited she reportedly said to the owners: "I have come from my house to your palace". The Italian revolutionary leader Giuseppe Garibaldi is thought to have been a guest here. The house is now owned by the Foreign Office and is usually closed to the public, but the interior can be seen in films including *The Young Victoria*, *The King's Speech*, and *The Importance of Being Earnest*.

As every Zimbabwean reader will know, the building was the scene of the Lancaster House Conference of 1979, in which Rhodesia's independence from Britain was negotiated.

To see a four-minute film of the house's interiors, search on YouTube for "London's West End's Royal Wedding Showcase at Lancaster House".

Walk a little further east to Stable Yard Road on your left. Again, the road is guarded but you can see Clarence House at the north end of the lane on the right.

Clarence House

View towards Clarence House, home of Prince Charles and "Camilla", the Duchess of Cornwall

Built in 1827, Clarence House has been lived in by a long list of royals including several of Queen Victoria's children. It was the home of the present queen's mother from 1953 until 2002. Now it is the home of Prince Charles and his wife, the Duchess of Cornwall. According to newspaper reports "Camilla", as she is popularly called, moved into Clarence House with Charles in 2003 and, like a true nestmaker, redecorated immediately, although the couple were only married two years later.

Walk west along The Mall to the roundabout in front of Buckingham Palace, then to Canada Gate on the roundabout's north side.

Canada Gate and the Canada Memorial

The Canadian government commissioned the Canada Gate as a memorial to Queen Victoria. It is in the same style as the gates of Buckingham Palace, which were built at the same time. On the gates are the emblems of the seven Canadian provinces at that time.

About 100 metres north-west of Canada Gate is the Canada Memorial, made from red stone with Canadian maple leaves carved into it. It was opened by Queen Elizabeth in 1994 in memory of the thousands of Canadian soldiers who died in two world wars.

Canada Gate, a gift from the Canadian government

Canada Memorial, in memory of Canadian war dead

The gateway where The Mall joins the roundabout is known as Africa Gate, and the gate to the south of the roundabout is Australia Gate.

Buckingham Palace

Turn now to look at the roof of Buckingham Palace. Most British people think that if the British flag is flying, the Queen is at home, but this is not the case. The British flag means the Queen is away; the Royal Standard flag, which features seven lions and an Irish harp, means she is in the palace. Even when at home, however, she is not usually available to ordinary visitors, so you will only be able to visit her today if you are the president or prime minister of your country.

At the front of Buckingham Palace is the balcony where Royal Family members sometimes appear at times of national celebration; the most recent occasion was immediately following the wedding of Prince William and Catherine Middleton. The Mall was full of crowds waiting for the newly-weds to appear, and there were excited shouts of "We want Kate". When the happy couple finally appeared there was great demand from the crowds for a royal kiss, and they got two – that is, they saw two. The first lasted 0.76 seconds; the second was a much more sensual 1.25 seconds. The watchers were delighted, except for a three-year-old bridesmaid on the balcony who covered her eyes. If you are a little more romantic than that young lady you can witness the kisses for

Buckingham Palace

The world's most famous palace was built in 1701 but only became the official residence of the monarch when Queen Victoria was crowned in 1837. Since then many monarchs have lived there and the palace has been visited by hundreds of foreign leaders.

Buckingham Palace is not just a house for the Royal Family; it is more like a small town. Around 800 people work in the building's 92 offices, and there is a post office, a cinema, a swimming pool and a doctor's surgery.

Over 40,000 light bulbs are used in the palace, and there are over 350 clocks and watches in the building, with two members of staff needed to keep them in good working order.

At the back of Buckingham Palace is the largest private garden in London, which contains a tennis court, a small lake and a helipad. Pop and classical music concerts are sometimes held there, and garden parties take place during the summer.

Buckingham Palace. The Royal Standard flag is flying, which means the Queen is at home

yourself by searching on YouTube for "William and Kate Kiss on the Balcony - The Royal Wedding - BBC".

Go to the south-east of the Queen Victoria statue in front of Buckingham Palace and look down into St James's Park. Set into the pathway is a round plaque with a rose in the centre and, around the outer edge, the words THE DIANA PRINCESS OF WALES MEMORIAL WALK. This walk was opened in 2000 as a tribute to Diana, and passes several parks and five houses where Diana lived or which were important in her life.

Plaque from the Diana Princess of Wales Memorial Walk

At this point you may want to walk west to see two further sights: the Royal Mews, where the Queen's carriages and cars are kept; and the extremely "posh" Goring Hotel, where Catherine Middleton has stayed. These two attractions will add about 20 minutes to your walk. Otherwise, jump ahead to the description of St James's Park.

From Buckingham Palace take Spur Rd south, then follow Buckingham Palace Rd until you see the Royal Mews on your right.

The Royal Mews

The Royal Mews, where the royal cars, carriages and horses are kept

The meaning of the word "mews" has changed over the years. Originally it meant a place where falcons and other hunting birds were kept. The Royal Mews was formerly in Charing Cross, where Trafalgar Square is now, and when it burnt down in 1534 it was rebuilt as a stables but the name was kept, which is why "mews" came to mean stables. Nowadays a "mews" usually means a quiet back street of stables that have been converted to houses, which is something found mostly in London but also in Canada and the USA (Washington Mews in New York is an example).

London mews properties are usually quiet oases amid the noise of city life. If you would like to see a typical example, directions to the nearest one will be given after the Goring Hotel.

The Royal Mews refers to the older meaning of the word "mews", that is,

stables. About 30 horses are kept here, together with the Royal Family's cars and coaches (carriages pulled by horse). The staff who look after the horses live in flats above the stables.

To see a five-minute video behind the scenes at the Royal Mews, go to YouTube and search for "The Royal Mews prepares for the Royal Wedding".

The Royal Mews can normally be visited Monday to Saturday from 10 am to 4 pm.

The Goring Hotel

Continue west along Buckingham Palace Rd then turn right into the peace and quiet of Victoria Square, where there is a statue of a young and innocent-looking Queen Victoria. Ian Fleming, writer of the James Bond novels, lived at no. 16. Turn left into Beeston Place, where you will see the Goring Hotel on your left.

The Goring Hotel, said to be a favourite of the Queen and Margaret Thatcher

The Goring is London's only family-owned luxury five-star hotel and is reputed to be a favourite of the Queen and Margaret Thatcher. Winston Churchill and President Dwight D Eisenhower have stayed here, as have many other famous guests, most notably Catherine Middleton and her family on the night before her wedding to Prince William.

To see a very relaxed-looking Catherine Middleton arriving at the Goring, Google

"Royal wedding: Kate Middleton arrives at Goring Hotel".

Amazing Goring facts include the following: the hotel opened in 1910, the first in the world with en suite bathrooms. In World War II the Allied Forces directed their military campaign from the hotel. Perhaps less importantly for the world, the cake for Prince Charles' christening in 1948 was baked by Goring chefs.

If you are dissatisfied with your accommodation in London you could consider moving to the five-room suite where Catherine Middleton's family stayed, although you may need to break your budget to afford it. A more wallet-friendly way to experience the Goring is to take afternoon tea there from 3.30 to 4.30 pm at the bargain price of £35 plus tip. Cheaper still is simply to stare through the windows to the left of the front door and watch the seriously rich and posh enjoying dinner.

There is a typical London mews one minute's walk away. To see it, go south down Beeston Place, cross the busy Grosvenor Gardens, and the first turning on your right is Mews North.

Follow your footsteps back to Buckingham Palace and continue to St James's Park.

St James's Park

Looking east over St James's Park

The Guards Museum and Toy Soldier Centre

St James's Park is the oldest royal park in London. It was created in 1603 on marshland by King James I, who used it to house exotic animals such as camels, crocodiles, an elephant and a collection of birds (see Birdcage Walk, below). Nowadays the most exotic creatures to be found there are a colony of pelicans descended from birds originally presented in 1664 by the Russian ambassador.

Walk around the park if you wish before going to the Guards Museum at the western end of Birdcage Walk.

Guards Museum

The Guards Museum is on Birdcage Walk, named for the Royal Aviary (a small zoo for birds) which was established there in the seventeenth century.

The museum itself is in Wellington Barracks, home to the five British Army regiments that are based here for the protection of the Royal Family. The museum tells the history of the regiments and the battles in which they participated. The museum shop is called The Guards Toy Soldier Centre, suggesting that the regiments find time for fun in their busy schedule.

Walk east along Birdcage Walk, continue into Great George St then immediately turn right and walk south down Storey's Gate, at the end of which is the western entrance of Westminster Abbey.

Westminster Abbey

Tradition says a church existed on this site from around the year 624, but construction of Westminster Abbey began in 1050.

The abbey has had a royal connection for centuries. 38 monarchs have been crowned here including the present queen in 1953, and numerous monarchs have been buried on the site, the earliest more than 1400 years ago, the long-forgotten Sæberht of Essex. At least 16 royal weddings have taken place at the abbey, most recently that of Prince William and Catherine Middleton in April 2011, one of the most widely-watched royal events ever. Around half the British population watched all or part of the wedding ceremony, and it was shown on television in 180 countries worldwide.

About 20 monarchs lie buried at the abbey, an honour shared by many famous writers and poets including Charles Darwin, William Shakespeare, Charles Dickens and Lord Byron.

Westminster Abbey is open from Monday to Saturday for visits and on Sunday for services.

Walk east along Broad Sanctuary to Parliament Square, then walk north then east to its north-east corner, then continue east along Bridge St to Westminster Station, where the walk ends.

Western door to Westminster Abbey

Market London

Start:	Aldgate East tube station (Aldgate tube station is nearby)
End:	Liverpool Street tube station
Length:	3.5 miles (5 kilometres)
Time taken:	2 hours plus shopping in markets
Eat and drink:	The best options are the Indian restaurants in Brick Lane and the international food halls in the Sunday Upmarket and the Boiler House
Includes:	Petticoat Lane Market, former Jewish Soup Kitchen, Sandy's Row Synagogue, Old Spitalfields Market, Brick Lane (London's Bangladeshi district), Bangla City supermarket, Sunday Upmarket, Backyard Market, Boiler House Food Hall, Brick Lane Food Village, Brick Lane Market, Columbia Road Flower Market
Best time:	Sunday morning, the only time when all the markets are open. The first and the last two markets - Petticoat Lane Market, Columbia Road Market and Brick Lane Market respectively - all end at around 2 pm on Sunday, so if you begin the walk after breakfast on Sunday you should have time to visit all the markets. If you want to take things slowly, you could simply leave the last two markets for another day, which will give you more time to shop and eat as you go

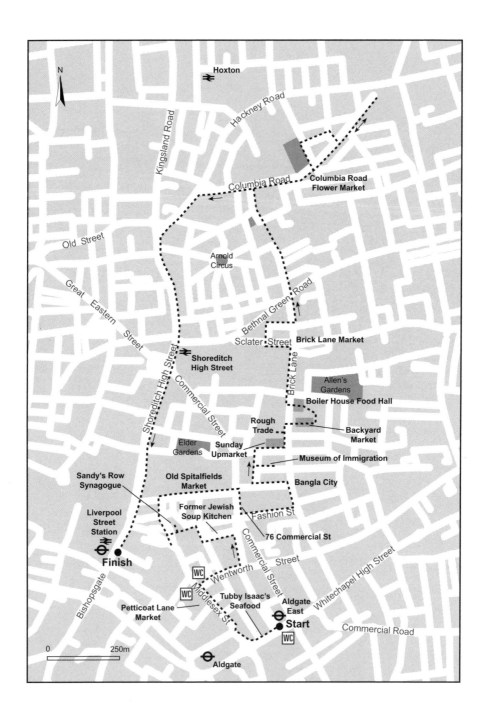

Introduction

There are hundreds of markets in London, of all types. Some are in specially-built market halls, some take place in the street; some specialise in one product type, others sell anything and everything; some are tourist-oriented, some are traditional; some are hundreds of years old, while others have appeared in the last few years; but all of them add colour and interest to their surrounding areas.

Many of London's markets first appeared in Victorian times because they were the quickest and cheapest way to provide food to people in new housing developments. Also, until cheap fridges became available, shoppers could not store fruit and vegetables so had to buy fresh food at nearby markets every day. But if their local area changes, markets can disappear quickly. Many have survived only by adapting to modern tastes, and in some cases have managed this so successfully that they have actually lifted the reputations (and house prices) of their local areas.

This walk takes us to several London markets which although near each other are totally different in character. The area we will visit, informally called the East End, was also known historically as an arrival point for London's immigrants, many of whom worked in the markets; and we will see some of the signs of their presence and the influences they have had on the area.

Walk

Petticoat Lane Market

Exit Aldgate East tube station into Whitechapel Rd, which because of a law passed in 1283, when this area was countryside, was built wide to make it harder for criminals to hide in bushes and attack passing travellers (famous highwayman Dick Turpin was once nearly captured in a pub a little way east along this road). The street was a "drove road", meaning that cattle were walked to market along it, which was another reason it remained wide. From the early 1600s the Whitechapel Hay Market was held here three times a week; it continued until

Petticoat Lane Market on Middlesex Street

1928, long after the area had ceased to be rural. It is said that at the end of a long day of hay-selling and beer-drinking the market-men climbed into their carts and slept while their horses pulled them all the way back to their farms in Essex with no guidance.

Walk west. On the corner of Goulston St note Tubby Isaac's, a seafood stand we will discuss later. **Continue west to Middlesex St, then turn right and walk north**, and you will soon see the clothes stalls of Petticoat Lane Market. **Go north till you reach some steps on your left that lead up to Petticoat Tower, just where Wentworth St joins Middlesex St, and walk up the steps for a good view of the market.** Our intention for each market is to take you to it, describe its origins and modern-day characteristics, and then leave you to explore it in your own time without referring constantly to this book.

To understand Petticoat Lane Market today we need to know a little of its past. The market has its origins in around 1608 when a second-hand clothes market was set up here, giving the street the name Petticoat Lane. A petticoat was originally a type of skirt but over the years it began to mean a piece of women's underwear, so the street's name was changed in 1830 (would you want to live in an Underpants St?); the market name remained, however.

The wide variety of unskilled jobs, low-cost housing and less regulation were all

London's East End

London was much smaller in the seventeenth century - the main part of the city stretched from a little way west of St Paul's Cathedral to around the Tower of London - so where you are now standing was then just outside London. The area east of London has always been relatively poor, partly because it was not always pleasant to live in. The Thames carried rubbish downstream from west to east, and it often flooded the land here, bringing disease with it (malaria existed in this area until the early twentieth century). Also, the air in the East End was dirtier - the wind most often blows from the west, carrying pollution from west to east (if you stand on top of London's Greenwich Hill you can actually see this happening).

As an aside, it is not just in London that the wind direction has made the west richer than the east; it is the same in almost every post-industrial town and city in England, including Bristol, Newcastle, Durham, Doncaster, Manchester, Wolverhampton, Sheffield, Derby, and many others. Google "mouseprice heatmap" (sic) to see how property prices are higher in the west of all those cities. The same pattern can be seen in many cities in mainland Europe.

So the rich of London preferred to live in the west, leaving the east for the "stink industries" such as the making of rope, brushes, cigarettes, guns, church bells, papers, glass, matches, baskets, and many types of food including sugar, a surprisingly smelly industry because historically it involved boiling animal blood and bones. The development of these businesses caused the building of cheap houses nearby, because there was little public transport then and people had to live near their place of work. Even after the area was completely urbanised, some people had small farms in their back gardens and yards for the keeping of cows, chickens, ducks and rabbits, which could be fed cheaply on old vegetables from the markets, grain from the breweries and hay from the Whitechapel Hay Market. Cows mostly disappeared from the area during World War II because they became terrified during bombing raids.

Bomb damage, population change and the rise in property prices have ended most of the manufacturing businesses in the East End, but a few survive - there are still two large sugar refineries, and the Whitechapel Bell Foundry still makes bells here in Britain's oldest factory.

factors that made the East End a suitable area for immigrants to London. It was in any case the arrival point for many of them – they stepped off their boats straight onto the docks of East London.

The first big "wave" of immigration to London was the arrival of around 40,000 French Huguenots in the late seventeenth century, at a time when London's population was only about 500,000. The Huguenots set up a large weaving (cloth-making) industry in the East End, and clothes have been made in the area ever since. The newcomers brought other useful skills such as watchmaking, printing, even the making of surgical instruments, and their economic success meant that they integrated easily into London society (by 1750 they no longer spoke French). Most of them moved on from this area long ago but have left their mark in many ways, as we will see.

By 1900 London's population was around 7 million, of whom around 30% were born abroad (those two figures are the same today). Whereas New York's story of immigration is widely understood and is physically preserved in the museum at Ellis Island, London's is much less known. In the last decades of the nineteenth century large numbers of people from Ireland, Germany, Italy and France came to London, as well as smaller numbers from China, India and elsewhere in the British Empire; but the greatest influx was the 150,000 Jews who arrived from Eastern Europe (see the River London walk, which takes you past the actual place where many of them first stepped onto British soil). Like the

Huguenots before them many Jews chose (or had no alternative) to live in this part of London and work in the clothing industry. If you had been here in 1900, virtually all the market stalls you see would have been Jewish-owned, as would most of the shops. Many of today's prominent British Jews or their parents grew up in this area, for example Jonathan Sacks, Britain's Chief Rabbi. Most of the area's Jewish population moved to north London in the decades after World War II, but not all; and we will see small signs of the Jewish presence in the area as we walk.

At least two prominent Jewish businessmen began their commercial careers on stalls in Petticoat Lane Market: Alan Sugar, founder of electronics company Amstrad; and Gerald Ratner, founder of jewellery company Ratners Group.

Gradually much of the area's Jewish population moved on to north London, in particular Golders Green, Hendon and Stamford Hill (the so-called "bagel belt"), and the East End was settled by yet another wave of immigrants, this time from South-east Asia, Bangladesh in particular, which we will discuss later. Their presence is especially visible further on in the walk, but Petticoat Lane too has its share of Bangladeshi shops and stalls.

In short, the history of Petticoat Lane Market reflects the history of the East End over the last few centuries, with different waves of immigrants involving themselves in the clothes trade and working in the market.

The clothes shops around Petticoat Lane Market mostly sell good-quality clothing, some of it made locally by the shop-owners' families. The market stalls however target the poorer residents of the area and generally sell on price rather than quality.

The market is not a tourist destination, except for more adventurous visitors, but because of its liveliness and diversity it is an excellent place to people-watch, and a good place to shop for cheap clothes.

Standing halfway up the steps and looking north as far as you can, you will see smart office buildings and skyscrapers on the west side of the road and much older and less clean buildings on the east side. This is because Middlesex St is the boundary line between the City of London, the capital's wealthy financial district, and Tower Hamlets, one of the poorest parts of London. The local saying is: when you're in the gutter (the edge of the road), you're in Tower Hamlets; when you're on the pavement, you're in the City. All the markets on this walk are just outside the City, for the reasons given.

One of a handful of remaining Jewish businesses in Middlesex Street

There are a few remaining Jewish businesses around the market. Underneath the steps where you are standing is a row of shops, most of which (according to the City of London Police's Neighbourhood Profile for Portsoken ward) are Jewish-owned.

Tubby Isaac's, which we saw near the start of the walk, is a Jewish business that started in 1919 and is still run by the same family. Along with seafood the stall sells jellied eels, thought of as a traditional East End dish. Eels were formerly common in the Thames and became a favourite of London's poor. They are a less fashionable food today, but enough loyal customers still remain to keep Tubby Isaac's in business. **Briefly walk west to the top of the stairs to see Petticoat Tower's open square**, which is much better looked-after

Tubby Isaac's, a Jewish seafood business started in 1919

than you might expect on a council estate. The reason for that is simple: the City of London can afford to throw money at it.

Look around the market, then walk north along Toynbee St (Arnold Toynbee was a Victorian social reformer; his grand-daughter Polly Toynbee is a well-known journalist). On your right is a block of shops, mysteriously derelict for many years.

At Brune St turn left and walk west. On your right is a former soup kitchen for the Jewish poor, now converted to flats. When it closed in 1994 it was still feeding around 100 elderly Jewish clients in the area.

Continue west and turn right at Tenter Ground. This short street's name is a reference to the area's Huguenot past. Huguenot weavers would stretch newly-made cloth on "tenterhooks" to prevent it from shrinking (getting smaller); at some time in the past this land was probably a field full of frames of drying cloth. The Victorian buildings on the street's west side are typical of the type of slum houses that once covered this whole area, which was 12 times more crowded than the richer parts of London, and it was common for whole families and even their animals to live in one small room.

At the end of Tenter Ground turn left, right, then left again and walk west along Artillery Lane. Do not follow the road where it bends north; instead continue west along Artillery Passage, an atmospheric narrow alley containing some fine historical shopfronts. **At the end of the passage turn left and walk a few metres south to the Indian restaurant on your left.** This building was once run by

Former soup kitchen for the Jewish poor

Historic shop fronts on Artillery Lane

Ayub Ali Master as a boarding-house for Bangladeshis; we will read more of him later. **Now walk a few metres north up Sandy's Row; on the right you will see Sandy's Row Synagogue at no. 4a.**

Sandy's Row Synagogue

The building at 4a Sandy's Row was built as a church in 1766 by French Huguenots. As the area's Huguenot population gradually moved away the building was taken over first by a succession of Baptist churches and then in 1867 by a community of Jews from Holland, who turned it into a synagogue. The interior's orange décor reflects the synagogue's Dutch origins, and some descendants of the original community are still members.

Sandy's Row Synagogue, one of the small number of synagogues still open in the East End

The building's original entrance was on the south-east side of the building. By tradition Jews pray in the direction of Jerusalem, which is south-east from London; so the front door was moved to the north-west side and the Torah scrolls were placed on the south-east wall of the building's interior. You can still see the blocked-up original entrance by going up Parliament Court, off Artillery Passage.

As the East End's Jewish population gradually moved away from the East End after World War II, most of the area's synagogues closed down, with only a small handful now remaining, and it was feared the building would have to close. In recent years, however, the synagogue has been welcoming new recruits through its doors. Many Jewish people work in the City, London's financial district, which is a short walk west of the synagogue, and so are able to attend lunchtime services. Additionally, young Jewish people are moving to the East End in increasing numbers because of its nearness to the City and relatively low house prices.

The synagogue's future has been further guaranteed by a grant of over £250,000 from English Heritage to carry out necessary renovation work. **Continue north up Sandy's Row, then cross Artillery Lane and continue north up Fort St. You will reach an open square, formerly a cemetery**, which now contains several sculptures, a pond and the ruined crypt of the Chapel of St Mary, preserved below ground level and explained fully on history boards.

Walk east on the south side of Brushfield St. No. 42 is A. Gold, now a delicatessen but in the 1880s a French

A Gold, high-quality English delicatessen in historic shop premises

milliner's owned by a Hungarian Jewish woman called Amelia Gold. When you see The Gun pub on the south side of Brushfield St, cross to the north side of the road, stand by the entrance to Old Spitalfields Market (with the chocolate shop just to your right) and look north into the market building.

Old Spitalfields Market

Interior of Old Spitalfields Market

A market has existed on this site since 1638, but the current market building was constructed in 1887 for a fruit and vegetable market. The market moved to a larger site in north London in 1991, after which the building stood mostly empty except for a very few market stalls on Sundays. In 2005, following several years of redevelopment, the site reopened in a modernised form. The market stalls are now found throughout the building, while in the western section are several restaurants. Smart shops are located around the edges of the market building.

Old Spitalfields Market and Petticoat Lane Market are only a short distance apart geographically but are completely different from each other. A street market like Petticoat Lane has no single physical building that can be invested in. Spitalfields, on the other hand, had an attractive Victorian market building that

could be used to house high-end shops and restaurants, all paying healthy rents, which made it a good investment for the developers.

Petticoat Lane Market is held only once a week, and therefore has only a limited effect on its surroundings. Spitalfields, open seven days a week, attracts a steady stream of well-off visitors who spend money on local shops and services, thereby helping to regenerate the area.

A further advantage Spitalfields has is that it is midway between Liverpool Street Station and the attractions of Brick Lane (which we will visit next), so there are a great many passers-by. Petticoat Lane is hidden away in a corner of London where there are no nearby attractions.

While standing by the Spitalfields market entrance looking north into the market building, you should see a row of restaurants on your left, market stalls directly in front of you, and a raised floor on your right with several restaurants on it. Look up to the roof. You can see that the Victorian roof ends where the raised floor ends; the roof to the west of that is newer. There are many further market stalls on the eastern side of the raised floor section.

Walk round the market at your leisure, then leave via the same southern entrance where you entered, and walk east, crossing Commercial St. The Ten Bells pub on the corner of Commercial St and Fournier St used to be the Jack The Ripper pub because of the murders committed near here in 1888, but in recent years a group of women who did not find the joke funny forced a change of name. Ahead of you is the imposing white stone of Christ Church Spitalfields. In *1902* Jack London, author of *Call of the Wild*, described the beggars who slept in the churchyard at night:

... full of rags and filth, every kind of disgusting disease, open wounds, indecency, monstrosities and animal-like faces. A freezing wind was blowing, and these creatures shivered there in their rags trying to sleep.
[transliterated into easier English]

Walk south on Commercial St past some underground toilets that are now converted to a bar. Pass on your left a drinking-fountain for humans and its zoological cousin on your right, a trough for horses to drink at – these were installed to provide clean water after the cholera epidemics of the nineteenth century. Pass no. 76 Commercial St, formerly the site of the first curry restaurant in the area; we will read more about it soon. **Turn left into Fashion St and walk east.** The south side of this street once led to dark alleyways and courts that were full of poverty and criminality, until they were knocked down and the long Moorish-style building was constructed in 1905. It was intended as a shopping arcade, but that plan failed and the building is now occupied by small businesses.

At the end of Fashion St is Brick Lane.

Brick Lane

Why is there a curry street in the East End, and why do most of the Bangladeshis who run it come from one particular part of Bangladesh? To answer that we need to go back to the early nineteenth century when the British East India Company controlled most of the Indian sub-continent including Sylhet, where they had a great number of tea plantations. When the first Anglo-Burmese war broke out in 1824, the British recruited thousands of Sylheti soldiers to fight the Burmese, and this was the start of the strengthening of ties between Britain and Sylhet.

Brick Lane, the heart of "Banglatown"

During peacetime, many of the independent-minded Sylhetis refused to participate in the dull routine of working on the tea plantations, to the annoyance of the British, who had to import labourers from other parts of India. The Sylhetis were independent landowners, but as the area's population grew the land became unable to support all of them and some began to look elsewhere for work. Although Sylhet is a mountainous region far from the sea, the connection with the British meant that Sylhetis were able to find work as sailors on British ships, and many did so. The first Bangladeshis to arrive in London came on British ships.

During World War I, thousands of Sylhetis were recruited to work on British naval ships. It was harsh and dangerous work, and on arrival in Britain some of them simply left their ships and started living around the docks of East London, a short walk south of where we are. The community slowly grew, and in 1938 a Sylheti named Ayub Ali Master opened a curry house, the Shah Jalal Restaurant, at no. 76 Commercial St, which we just passed. His restaurant soon became popular not just with London's Bangladeshis but also with Englishmen who had worked in colonial India and missed the food. Ayub Ali Master also owned 13 Sandy's Row, which we saw before, and he ran it as a lodging-house where Bangladeshis could stay. It soon became a sort of Bangladeshi community and advice centre which they referred to simply as "Number 13". Brick Lane developed from those early beginnings into the Bangladeshi residential and restaurant district that you now see.

Most British people do not know that around 90% of Britain's 8,500 "Indian" restaurants are owned and worked not by Indians but by Bangladeshis. When the first Indian restaurants were set up in Britain, the territory that is now Bangladesh was part of India, so "Indian" was the obvious description for the restaurants. After 1947, when Bangladesh separated from India, the British were so used to "Indian" food that the expression stuck.

Brick Lane

Brick Lane has in the last few years become one of London's most famous streets. It has been described as a place where "Eastern promise meets East End chaos". The "promise" is curry restaurants, art shows, new fashion brands and several lively markets. The "chaos", if that is the right word, is simply the crowds and the informality of the area.

Previously a Huguenot and then Jewish district, Brick Lane is now the lively centre of London's Bangladeshi community, most of whom are originally from the region of Sylhet in north-eastern Bangladesh.

Walk north on Brick Lane, stopping at any shops or restaurants that interest you. You may notice a surprising number of off-licences (alcohol shops). The Brick Lane restaurants are mostly owned by Muslims, some of whom are unwilling to serve alcohol, so they ask their customers to buy it elsewhere and bring it in to the restaurant.

When you reach Fournier St you may like to visit the Bangla City supermarket on the east side of Brick Lane; it contains a great many products not often seen in British shops. If you are in the mood for a snack now you could ask for Bombay mix, or variations of it including chevda mix, sev mamra, Gujarati mix or chevda mild, which because they are tasty and require no preparation are perfect as "nibbles" (a pre-meal snack), as you will find out if you ever come to dinner at your author's house.

Several types of dates are on sale at Bangla City. For something interesting that you can take away and eat later, the shop's plum chutney is recommended. Other interesting possibilities are tinned jackfruit, cardamom tea or date molasses. One thing you will not see on display is saffron; compared by weight it is more expensive than gold, and it is considered too risky to have it on open display; but the shop assistants bring it out to customers when asked.

Bangla City stands on the site of the former Russian Vapour Baths, visited by Jews before attending the synagogue on Friday evenings. The baths must have sentimental value for London's Jews because the building's sign is now in the Jewish Museum.

After Bangla City, stand on the corner of Fournier St and Brick Lane and look west.

Fournier St

Fournier St is part of the Wood-Michell estate, built between 1718 and 1728 and first occupied mostly by Huguenots. Although the houses here are often described as "weavers' houses", in fact they originally belonged to wealthy cloth merchants. However, when the weaving industry began to decline because of mechanisation and competition from France and the north of England, the merchants got into financial difficulty and many of them added garrets (attics) to the tops of their houses so they could rent them to weavers for extra income. Looking up, you can see the garrets were mostly designed with large windows to allow maximum light for the delicate work of weaving.

Eighteenth-century Huguenot silk merchants' houses on Fournier Street

On the north corner of Fournier St and Brick Lane is the London Jamme Masjid, a mosque with a controversial new metal minaret (tower) on its eastern side. Before that it was the Spitalfields Great Synagogue, and before that, La Neuve Eglise. As every student of London's immigrant history knows, the building thus neatly mirrors the area's demographic history, having been first a

Huguenot place of worship then a Jewish one and now an Islamic one.

Walk west along Fournier St. At no. 33 on the right is another reminder of the area's Jewish past, a heavily graffiti'ed

Silk-weaving in the East End

Weaving was not an easy profession. 12-14 hours of work a day was common, and weavers suffered from various physical problems caused by bending over their looms (weaving machines) all day, and from the lack of fresh air. The windows in their workshops were always closed to keep the air damp (wet), partly to prevent the silk thread from breaking but also so that the finished silk was heavier and appeared to be of more value.

Huguenots in London planted many mulberry trees in the hope of producing home-made silk, but Britain's cold climate made that idea unworkable. A "Mulberry St" in the East End marks the site of one of these attempts, and in fact one lonely mulberry tree still survives in a garden in Soho, another area of London where Huguenots settled. A Huguenot church exists in Soho to this day, founded in 1550 and still serving London's French Protestants in French.

A few silk-weavers survived in this part of London until well into the twentieth century - photographs exist of very elderly Huguenots weaving silk in the East End as late as the 1930s - but none were in business by the beginning of World War II. However, the East End silk-weaving story is by no means dead. In the nineteenth century several of the area's silk firms moved to towns outside London where costs and taxes were lower, for example Sudbury in Suffolk, and some of those firms still exist, though today they weave by machine rather than on hand looms. Sudbury is Britain's "silk capital", with four firms still producing high-quality silk. The town contains some interesting weaving-related buildings including workshops, factory shops and weavers cottages.

London Jamme Masjid mosque, in a former Huguenot church building

garage door with "S. Schwartz" painted above, by an unknown signwriter who painted many signs in the area.

Turn right into Wilkes St then right again into Princelet St. On the ground outside no. 8 on the right is a metal plaque showing a violin, marking the former site of the Yiddish Theatre, built in 1886 for the great Jewish actor Jacob Adler. During a performance in 1887 the audience rushed to the exit thinking (wrongly) that the building was on fire, and seventeen people were crushed to death, following which the theatre closed down. Jacob Adler, like many other London Jews, moved on to America and became a founder of the American Yiddish theatre tradition, which – to cut a very long story very short – eventually developed into the American film industry, in other words, "Hollywood". Adler's six children all became actors, and his daughter Stella taught acting to a long list of stars including Marlon Brando, Judy Garland and Robert De Niro. Your author feels sure that when you walked into this street you were not expecting it to have any connection with Hollywood.

A little further east is no. 19 Princelet St, originally the home of a Huguenot silk merchant. In 1869 it was converted into a synagogue, but is now the as-yet under-developed Museum of Immigration and

19 Princelet Street, former synagogue and now home to the seldom-open Museum of Immigration

Diversity, which because of the building's structural weaknesses is only open for a few days every year.

Return west to Wilkes St and walk north to Hanbury St, then turn right and walk east. At no. 22 is Hanbury Hall, first a Huguenot Chapel then owned by other religious groups including the Church of England. In 1888 Karl Marx's daughter Eleanor protested here against poor working conditions in the East End. It is now a community centre, and on Saturdays and Sundays a small vintage clothing fair is held here.

Continue east to Brick Lane, and when you reach it stop and look to the north. On both sides of the road are the former premises of the Black Eagle Brewery, now renamed the Old Truman Brewery.

Old Truman Brewery

The Old Truman Brewery is home to several of the markets we have come to see.

A brewery was established on this site in 1669, drawing the necessary water from deep wells, and quickly became a success. In the mid-eighteenth century Huguenot immigrants introduced a new type of beer made from fermented hop plants. Initially the hops were imported from Belgium but farmers in Kent (south of London) soon saw the market need and began to grow hops themselves. For many years working-class East Londoners travelled to Kent every summer in special "hop trains" for a hop-picking holiday. The custom ended in the 1950s when hop-picking was mechanised but it is looked back on nostalgically by many older Londoners today.

To watch a five-minute silent film about the hop holidays, Google "hop pickers off to Kent British Pathe").

Huguenot success in Britain

Not all Huguenots were satisfied with a silk-weaving career. In 1794 a George Courtauld became bored with sitting at his loom all day and thought there had to be something better. He was right - there was. He set up his own clothing company, which within a few decades had become one of the largest makers of clothes in Britain. Today it employs thousands of people in the UK and abroad, and is one of Marks and Spencer's biggest suppliers. In fact there is a very strong possibility that the underwear you are wearing were manufactured by them (a statement that your author is basing on statistics, not visual evidence).

Nowadays the Courtauld name is most widely known from the Courtauld Institute of Art in London, which the family founded with the donation of their large art collection - perhaps they were tired of being famous just for underwear. Its gallery can be visited:
http://www.courtauld.ac.uk/gallery

John Dollond was another dynamic eighteenth-century Huguenot who with his son Peter became a maker of optical instruments. Today their company is Dollond and Aitchison, with 2,500 employees and 480 branches across Britain. Other people of Huguenot descent you may know include, to list just a few with what are clearly French names, novelist Daphne du Maurier, musician Simon Le Bon, actor Laurence Olivier, the Fabergé jewellery family, and tailor's grandson Joseph Bazalgette, whom we meet in the River London walk as the builder of London's sewers.

The Old Truman Brewery on Brick Lane, now home to markets and a thriving arts scene

As Britain's rail and road networks improved in the nineteenth century the Black Eagle Brewery was able to distribute its produce all over the country and became famous nationwide.

However, other breweries started to compete, particularly those in Staffordshire where the water was ideal for brewing, and the Black Eagle Brewery went into a long period of decline, finally closing in 1988. But the buildings still stand, and have now been converted for use by several lively markets and other small businesses.

Sunday Upmarket

The Sunday Upmarket is in the building just to your left as you look north. Its 140 stalls specialise in jewellery, crafts, interiors and clothing. Most of the clothing stalls in the market are run by designer-makers, that is, people who have designed and made the clothes they are selling. The market has a reputation for "edgy" and "fashionable" bespoke items.

Your author is a well-travelled person of extreme intelligence, wide education, perfect manners and film-star good looks, as his friends and family will tell you. But he knows nothing about clothing or fashion, again as his friends and family will tell you. To tell the truth, he does not really know which clothes are "edgy" and "fashionable" and which are not, and he uses them to describe the clothes in the Sunday Upmarket only because everyone else does. He feels certain that you, the reader, know more about clothes than he does, and he asks that you visit the market and make your own judgements.

Your author is however very well qualified to discuss food, having eaten a minimum of three large meals every day of his life, and can confidently recommend the Sunday Upmarket's colourful and varied food area, which you can probably see through steamed-up windows to your left. Most of the stallholders cook the food in front of you, guaranteeing its freshness. Cuisines on offer include Ethiopian, Lithuanian, Thai, Argentine, Venezuelan, Mexican, Caribbean and too many more to mention, making the job of choosing your lunch a pleasantly difficult one. Of course, each stallholder will try to help you decide. If you dislike being pressurised, our helpful advice is to buy a meal and hold it in front of you as you walk round the food stalls, giving the impression that your choice has already been made.

Lithuanian food stall in the Sunday Upmarket

Most of the stalls charge around £5 for a full main course including meat, vegetables and salad. In case you think that seems like a lot for "street food", try comparing it to the cost of a restaurant meal plus drinks and tips, against which £5 seems like good value.

Downstairs in the building's basement is another vintage market, with second-hand clothing, sunglasses and other accessories.

Continue a short way north to Dray Walk on your left ("drays" are carts pulled by horses, formerly used here by the brewery. Carlsberg still call their delivery trucks "city drays"). More clothes shops are to be found in this road, as is Britain's largest music shop Rough Trade East, located in a warehouse where the beer Stella Artois was formerly brewed. Inside is a large collection of CDs, LP records and even seven-inch singles, plus a cafe and a young crowd enjoying it all.

The Backyard Market in Brick Lane

Exotic cuisines on offer in the Boiler House Food Hall

The Rough Trade music shop in Dray Walk

Walk east back to Brick Lane. A short way north is the Backyard Market, at the end of a walkway on your right.

Backyard Market

Like the Sunday Upmarket, the Backyard Market features many designer-makers, but as well as clothes has stalls selling arts and crafts, home-made food, hairdressers, leather goods and watches.

After seeing the stalls, walk to the north-east corner of the market hall and go through the door into the former brewery's yard. Walk north through the

yard and you will see in its north-west corner an outdoor eating area. Walk through that into the Boiler House Food Hall, full again of exotic cuisines including Polish, Cuban, Vietnamese, Sri Lankan, Malaysian, Moroccan, Korean and others. Now, read the next sentence carefully. The Sunday Upmarket has eating space but the Boiler House has seating space. There are chairs and tables both within the building and in the outside seating area you have just walked through (note that the meals get cold quite quickly outside).

The round structure in the centre of the hall is the base of the great chimney that towers above the whole area.

Back on Brick Lane

Back on Brick Lane, continue north. Just after Quaker St are still more young and edgy (that unavoidable word) clothes shops. At no. 170 on your right is Taylor's Yard, whose sign still has Hebrew lettering; apparently a Morris Berger ran a Jewish wood business on this site.

Carrom boards in Brick Lane

A little further north on the left is a set of carrom boards set up in the street, usually with Asian men enjoying a game. Carrom is something like a combination of chess and billiards, and although of Asian origin it has variants in many countries including the Baltic States and the USA. www.carrom.org has the rules, if you want to stop and try to show the locals how it's done.

Further food stalls line both sides of the road here; this section of the street is called the Brick Lane Food Village. **Continue under the railway line. North of that is Brick Lane Market.**

Brick Lane Market

Brick Lane Market

Like Petticoat Lane Market, Brick Lane Market established itself here just outside the City of London because rents were lower. For years it has been a traditional East End second-hand market, and much of that feel remains, though there are increasingly signs that the section on Brick Lane itself is gentrifying (becoming more fashionable).

On the right is Cheshire St, whose south side has attractive Victorian shop fronts housing designer stores, usually with cheap and cheerful market stalls in front. **Go west along Sclater St about 50 metres and stand between the two market yards**, one on each side of the road. Both are rather like "car boot sales", offering a huge variety of second-hand items such as bicycles, ancient DVD players, computers and tools, but also with some good-quality books at very low prices, and collectors' items such as stamps, coins and postcards.

Stalls on Sclater Street, former location of Club Row Animal Market

At the time of writing, a "bicycle mafia" exists which apparently steals bicycles late on Saturday nights and sells them at Brick Lane Market the next morning. Your author knows personally of one case where a bicycle owner learned on Sunday morning that his bicycle had been stolen, and came straight here and immediately saw it for sale. There was an unpleasant scene that lasted for 40 dramatic minutes until the police arrived and returned the bicycle to its owner.

Until 1983 the southernmost of the two yards was home to Club Row Animal Market, and you would have heard and smelt it long before you saw it. Most of the animals on offer were dogs, sometimes of doubtful cleanliness and health – wounds and sores were often covered up with black shoe polish.

Like much else on this walk, Club Row Animal Market originated with Huguenot immigrants, who brought from France two main passions: flowers and birds (on the Île de la Cité in central Paris there is still a flower market that on Sundays sells birds). If you had walked through the Huguenot districts of London at the height of the silk trade, you would have heard birds singing inside almost every house. Club Row Market originally sold birds such as canaries, pigeons, and parrots but later expanded to include other animals such as dogs and cats, and even goats, foxes and eagles.

Club Row Market finally closed because of the local council's worries over disease and the unhealthy condition of many of the animals. To see a short news clip of the market from the 1940s, Google "pathe dogs club row".

Explore the southernmost yard first – it has some old-fashioned wheeled wooden market carts falling to pieces in its north-east corner – then the northern yard, then walk east along Bacon St, with its untidy second-hand shops.

Visitors may not have many more years to see this old-fashioned second-hand side

of Brick Lane Market. The area is fast gentrifying because of changing tastes, increasing tourist traffic, and, most of all, the nearness of the City, whose wealth must one day spread into this traditionally poor neighbourhood.

Continue north up Brick Lane, past the two bagel shops and the Swedish bar on the left, till you reach Bethnal Green Rd, where the market ends.

Long-standing bagel shop on Brick Lane

If you still have enough physical and mental energy for one further market, the flowers of Columbia Rd await. Continue north across Bethnal Green Rd (the old Roman road from London to Colchester in Essex) and walk for five minutes (or perhaps ten, if your stomach is carrying too many of the exotic cuisines we saw earlier) to Columbia Rd, where you will see the market on your right. Long before you reach it you will probably see people walking away from the market carrying huge potted plants, like a scene from Day of the Triffids.

Stop by the pub The Birdcage at the western end of the market.

Second-hand furniture shop on Bacon Street

Columbia Road Market

Columbia Road Market began in 1869 as a general food market, and was originally held on weekdays inside a market hall, like that of Spitalfields. However, most of the traders disliked the market hall's rules and regulations, and many moved outdoors to trade in the street. Their places in the hall were taken by furniture makers, most of whom were Jewish. Because they did not want to trade on Saturday, permission was given for the market to open every Sunday, which was also useful for the fruit and vegetable traders of Spitalfields and Covent Garden, who sold the week's leftover stock here on Sundays. Eventually the market hall building was demolished, and many of the weekday stalls closed or moved elsewhere, but the Sunday stalls survive to this day, now specialising in flowers.

Looking west along Columbia Road

It is not in every city that the poorer areas display such a liking for flowers. The fact that they do in London is because – again – of the Huguenots, whose two interests of flowers and birds (as reflected in the name of the pub where you are standing) have – apologies – implanted themselves in East End culture. Many of the houses in the area around Columbia Rd have small but very well-tended gardens, filled with purchases from the flower market.

Although Columbia Rd Market is not in a wealthy area and not near any other tourist sites or even a tube station, it is thriving today. The Victorian-era shops that line Columbia Rd, once home to Jewish furniture-makers, are all independent, one of the last streets in London where this is the case. The road is cobbled and the lamp posts scream "Dickensian". The street architecture is so authentically Victorian that it is often used as a location for period films.

The street itself is packed tight with flower sellers. Competition for pitches (places for stalls) is high, and stallholders lose their pitch if they do not come often enough. Some stalls have been in families for generations, and many stallholders grow the produce they sell.

Interestingly, unlike other markets the stallholders at Columbia Road are almost all traditional East End Londoners with the accents and the loud but friendly sales technique you might expect, well developed from years of flower-selling. The shops on either side of the road, however, are mostly unconnected to flowers in any way, simply selling novelty and gift items.

One relatively recent development at Columbia Road is the many buskers (street musicians) performing around the market, mostly playing "easy listening" American songs. They are such good performers that you might think they are specially selected, like those at Covent Garden Market, but according to the Columbia Road Traders Association this is not the case.

Street musicians at Columbia Road Flower Market

Walk east along Columbia Road, and when you have finished looking at the street, **go north on Ezra St, which takes you to a small square. Off the north-east corner is Horatio St**, where a small restaurant serves fresh oysters, formerly a favourite food of London's poor. **Walk west along Ezra St**, where there are several more interesting shops and yards.

As we prepare to leave Columbia Rd Market its main disadvantage becomes clear – it is some distance to the nearest tube station (or perhaps that has saved it from being even more crowded). **Walk west towards Hackney Rd**. When you pass a nursery school on your right, notice the Victorian iron railings outside it. These are all that is left of the original Columbia Road market building

Victorian railings – all that remains of the original Columbia Road market building

Go west to Hackney Rd, continue west to Shoreditch High St, then walk south. You are on the old Roman road which connected London with northern England.

Just before you reach the bridge which crosses the road, you will see Boxpark on your left. Occupying disused railway lands, Boxpark is a shopping centre made from shipping containers, and hosts a number of tiny but fashionable clothes shops. Because it was quick and relatively cheap to create, it is low-risk, and will probably be widely copied if it is successful.

A similar sight is Container City, a few miles east of here. It is virtually a small town by the River Thames, but made almost completely out of containers. Some are residential, some are workshops and some are artists' studios.

The bridge beside Boxpark carries a railway line which has been completely enclosed in concrete, so that building work can take place safely all around the area without the railway line needing to close. **Continue south under the bridge**, where on Sundays you may see a small

Boxpark – a shopping centre made from old shipping containers

and very informal market, with street traders setting out a few cheap items on the pavement. It is presumably not legal but is apparently tolerated by police because of its out-of-the-way location.

Continue south, passing on your left the Damascu Bite, a Syrian eatery promising you a "totaly new experiance". Looking at the view on the right-hand side of the street as you walk south, try to guess where Tower Hamlets, the poorest part of London, ends, and the City of London, one of the richest areas in the world, begins. If you want to know, the border is marked by Worship St on the right, where the tired Victorian shops give up and the gleaming modern office buildings immediately take over.

For centuries the area you have just walked through was the refuge of the poor, the desperate and the newly-arrived, whether Huguenot, Irish, Jewish, Bangladeshi or whatever else. Today, the newest immigrants to the area are none of those – they are young British people who like the East End's history, its variety and its mix of cultures. But of course if they move here in great numbers, and if the City's office buildings spread ever further eastwards, there is a risk they will change or even destroy what makes the area unique. Your author hopes and believes the chain stores will be kept out and the markets will survive. Do this walk again in 20 years and see!

Continue south to Liverpool Street tube station on your right, where the walk ends.

Shopping London 1

Start and end:	Piccadilly tube station
Length:	1 mile (1.5 kilometres)
Time taken:	1 hour plus shopping time
Eat and drink:	Fortnum & Mason is high-quality but is not a cheap option. There are lower-cost restaurants along the south side of Piccadilly. The affordable restaurants of Chinatown are a short walk from Piccadilly tube station
Includes:	Fortnum and Mason (famous department store), Burlington Arcade, Royal Arcade, shops of St James, shops of Jermyn St, Piccadilly Arcade, Tramp night club, Princes Arcade
Best time:	During shopping hours, i.e. between 9 am and 5 pm Monday to Saturday

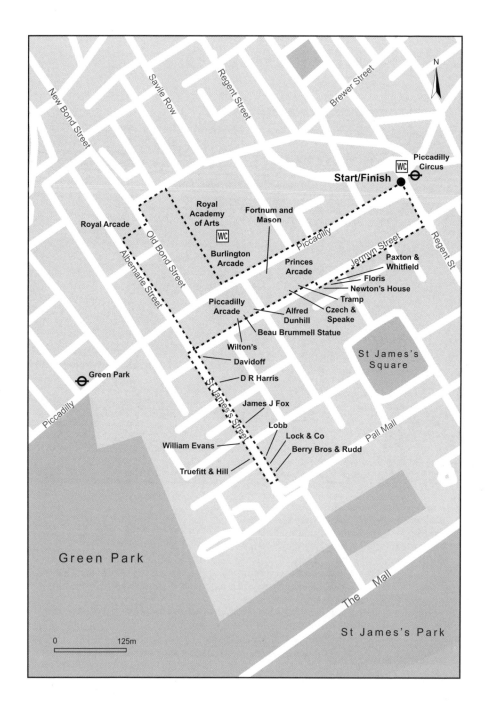

Introduction

If you hoped to see shops in London, you will not be disappointed – the city has more than 40,000 that together sell virtually everything imaginable, making London a popular shopping destination for visitors from all over Britain and the entire world.

Naturally London has most of the big international shop brands found in all countries, but a surprising number of smaller, more old-fashioned and traditionally "English" shops still survive. Sometimes eccentric but often charming, these little gems are reminders of a pre-chain-store era when personal and respectful service was worth more than a shiny international brand.

Many members of the Royal Family are customers of the shops in this walk. If you have ever wondered where Winston Churchill bought his cheese, where Princess Diana bought her chocolates or where Prince Philip, the Queen's husband, has his hair cut, by the end of the walk your curiosity will be satisfied.

This walk can be enjoyed without buying anything. The shop fronts are interesting to see even if you do not enter, and the whole area that the walk covers has a charmingly traditional feel that is worth experiencing.

Walk

From Piccadilly Circus underground station take exit number 2 (north side) and walk west along Piccadilly past St James's Church on your left (built in 1684 by Christopher Wren, who also designed St Paul's Cathedral).

St James's Church on Piccadilly

Fortnum & Mason

Fortnum & Mason preparing for Christmas

Continue to 181 Piccadilly, the department store Fortnum & Mason, on the south side of the road. Founded as a small shop in 1707 by servants in the royal household, the business grew as international trade led to the import of exotic products like teas and spices, which Fortnum's was among the first to sell. Since then the business has supplied many members of the Royal Family.

Above the store's doorway is a large clock added in 1964. Every hour on the hour, large models of the founders, William Fortnum and Hugh Mason, appear and bow to each other to the sound of eighteenth-century music.

Fortnum's is best-known for its five restaurants and its food, especially its range of tea. The store's luxury hampers (baskets of food) can be delivered all over the world.

As with all the shops mentioned on this walk, you are welcome to enter Fortnum's and browse or buy, or have a meal or snack.

Continue west along Piccadilly's north side. On your right, just after **Burlington House** (a former aristocratic mansion, now home to the Royal Academy of Arts and other academic societies) is Burlington Arcade, visible through an archway.

Burlington Arcade

Burlington Arcade was built in 1819 by Lord George Cavendish, the resident of Burlington House, to prevent the irritatingly disrespectful lower classes from throwing rubbish over the side wall of his garden. The arcade's style has influenced other nineteenth-century covered arcades in Brussels and Milan, and even led to the development of modern shopping centres.

Entrance to Burlington Arcade

The world's smallest police force operates in Burlington Arcade. Since the arcade opened the so-called "beadles" have enforced an ancient set of rules that forbid whistling, singing, playing music, and much more. You may see a beadle in traditional dress in the arcade – especially if you break any of the rules! Even the opening of umbrellas in the arcade is theoretically forbidden, as are babies' push-chairs, apparently to make stealing more difficult, though these rules are not always enforced.

The arcade can be seen in the 1996 film *101 Dalmatians*, when protagonist Roger is dragged on a bicycle by his dog at top speed through the arcade, past a shocked shoe-cleaner and an angry beadle, finally ending up in the pond at St James's Park. If there was not an arcade rule specifically forbidding that at the time, there surely is now.

To see the film clip concerned, search on YouTube for "101 Dalmatians 1996 Part 2".

Among the shops in the arcade are, in order as we walk north:

70 (right), Luponde Tea – tea shop of the Luponde organic tea estate in Tanzania. Wide range of attractive teapots and teacups.

12-13 (left side), Thomas Lyte – luxury goods made in London from leather and silver, including high-quality sporting trophies.

16-17 (left), Penhaligon's – distinctive perfumes in traditional Victorian-style bottles, made in England since 1870.

54-55 (right), Globe-Trotter – makers since 1897 of high-quality suitcases, used by Captain Scott on his Antarctic expedition in 1912, Edmund Hillary while climbing Everest in 1953, and by Winston Churchill and Queen Elizabeth II.

51 (right), Sermoneta – leather gloves for weddings, driving or special occasions.

24 (left), Vintage Watch Company – vintage Rolex watches from 1910 to 1970.

34 (left), Penfriend – sellers and repairers of modern and restored antique pens. Founded in 1950. SPECIAL OFFER: Penfriend are kindly offering a 5% discount on all modern pens except Montblanc to customers who bring this book with them.

Leave the arcade at its north end and turn left into Burlington Gardens, then left again into Old Bond St, and walk south till you see the Royal Arcade on your right.

Royal Arcade

Entrance to the Royal Arcade off Albemarle Street

The Royal Arcade opened in 1879, originally called simply The Arcade, as the old sign above shows. It was renamed when Queen Victoria became a customer of one of the shops. The arcade features a beautiful ceiling and a saddled glass roof.

Recommended shops in the Royal Arcade are:

1-2 (left), Charbonnel et Walker – makers of high-class chocolates since 1875, and one of the original tenants in the arcade. The Queen is a customer.

12 (right), Ormond Jayne – tiny perfumery specialising in little-used ingredients.

7 (left), William Weston Gallery – dealers in European and British Master prints.

Exit the arcade at its western end into Albemarle St, turn left and walk south, then cross Piccadilly into St James's St. We will walk downhill on the east side of the street then back uphill on the west side, passing as we go the shops below.

Davidoff (no. 35)

The Davidoff family tobacco business began in Kiev in the nineteenth century, and expanded in Switzerland during the Second World War. In 1968 the company launched its own brand of cigars using tobacco from the Dominican Republic.

D R Harris (no. 29)

One of London's oldest pharmacies, dating back over 200 years. A supplier to Prince Charles.

James J Fox (no. 19)

Founded in 1787 in this street. Formerly suppliers to Winston Churchill, Oscar Wilde and many other famous names.

Lobb (no. 9)

Lobb's is one of the oldest and most prestigious shoe shops in London, having provided hand-made shoes to a long list of celebrities including Frank Sinatra, Dean Martin, Aristotle Onassis, George Bernard Shaw and many world leaders. Members of the Royal Family are customers of Lobb, and the premises were visited in 2009 by Prince Charles and the Duchess of Cornwall. In its cellars the shop keeps 30,000 lasts (models of feet for shoe-making) for individual customers. Its shoes take six months to make and are aimed at wealthy clients – expect to pay £2500 for leather shoes and over £8000 for crocodile shoes.

Lock & Co (no. 6)

Lock was established in 1676 to provide hats for royal staff at the nearby St James's Palace. According to tradition, when an aristocrat walked in and shouted "Hat!", the shop staff had to place a suitable hat on his head before the echoes of his shout had died away. Admiral Lord Nelson was a customer.

Berry Bros & Rudd (no. 3)

Britain's oldest wine merchants, in operation from these premises since 1698. The shop is still owned by members of the original families, and, as you will see if you enter, has many antique features. Queen Elizabeth II and Prince Charles are among its customers, and it has won many wine-related awards.

The shop front is small but underground there are huge cellars that hold over 200,000 bottles of wine. Most are for sale but some are being left to mature. The cellars extend far out under the pavement and behind the shop. Usually the only way to see them is to book a place on one of Berry Bros' wine-tasting or gourmet dinner events which take place under the shop.

Truefitt & Hill (no. 71, west side)

Truefitt & Hill, founded in 1805, claim to be the world's oldest firm of barbers, and have the honour of cutting the hair of Prince Philip, husband of the Queen.

William Evans (no. 67)

Gentlemen's gunmakers, established in 1883. You will need a licence to make a purchase.

As you walk up St James's St you will notice a section in the centre of the road where taxis wait. Until the 1920s horse-drawn cabs waited in the same place.

Near the top of St James's St turn right and walk east into Jermyn St. It will be immediately clear why this street is known as a gentlemen's shopping destination: it contains a great many men's clothing and shoe shops, cigar shops and barbers. We will walk east along the street passing as we go a great many well-dressed men, and the following shops:

Wilton's (no. 55)

Traditional British restaurant originally established in 1742 as an oyster stall. Now popular with government ministers, aristocrats, film stars and businesspeople. Jacket required for men.

Beau Brummell Statue

Not a shop, but relevant to clothes shopping. George Brummell was a

nineteenth-century leader of fashion who claimed he spent five hours every day getting dressed. One of the characters in the musical *Cats*, the well-dressed Bustopher Jones, is referred to a "Brummell of cats".

Piccadilly Arcade

Beside the Brummell statue is the entrance to the Piccadilly Arcade, built in 1909. The good news is that it has no beadles, so you may open as many umbrellas and push as many prams in this arcade as you like.

Shops to be found there include, in order as we walk north:

23 (both sides), New & Lingwood – menswear. The business opened in the town of Eton in 1865 to serve pupils at Eton College, one of Britain's oldest and most prestigious private schools. After leaving school many former pupils loyally continue to support the company at its Jermyn St branch.

17 (right side), The Armoury – military medals and traditional-style toy soldiers.

15 (right side), St. James's Art Books – graphics, drawings and oil paintings.

8 (left), Snap Galleries – dealers in rare rock 'n' roll photographs.

5 (right), Iconastas – ancient and modern Russian art.

1 (right), Santa Maria Novella – one of the oldest pharmacy companies in the world, established in 1612 by Dominican friars. Products include face creams, bubble bath, tanning products, scented candles, liqueurs and honeys.

Back on Jermyn St, continue east to Alfred Dunhill.

Alfred Dunhill (no. 48)

Alfred Dunhill makes luxury products for men, including pens, watches and clothing. Several of the company's products have appeared in James Bond films, including cufflinks, cigarette lighters and the suit that Daniel Craig wears in *Casino Royale.*

The shop has its own free museum downstairs, which tells the story of the company's history. Among the items on display are Dunhill pipes, watches, fragrances, vanity cases, pens and historic cigarette lighters owned by famous people including Picasso, Harpo Marx, Noel Coward, Marshal Tito and Elvis Presley.

Tramp (no. 40)

Tramp is named for Charlie Chaplin (a "tramp" is a w a n d e r i n g homeless person), and is one of the most exclusive nightclubs in the world. It has welcomed the Beatles, the Rolling Stones, Frank Sinatra, Elton John, Muhammad Ali, Jack Nicholson, Paris Hilton, and a great many more famous names. Open only to members and their guests.

Czech & Speake (no. 39)

Makers of high-quality bathrooms and toiletries.

Princes Arcade

The most interesting shop in this arcade is luxury chocolate-maker Prestat, founded in 1902 in France. The Queen is a customer, as was Princess Diana. The store's wares feature in Roald Dahl's book

My Uncle Oswald, in which a femme fatale travels across Europe seducing (taking to bed) monarchs and great artists using Prestat chocolates.

Cross to the south side of Jermyn St.

Newton's House (no. 87)

On the building of no. 87 Jermyn St is a plaque marking the former home of the scientist Isaac Newton.

Floris (no. 89)

Luxury fragrances for men and women. The business has supplied its products to the monarchy since 1730.

Paxton & Whitfield (no. 93, south side)

Winston Churchill said that a gentleman would buy his cheese only at this shop. It has existed since 1742, and provided cheese to Queen Victoria in the nineteenth century. You are welcome to enter the shop and taste some of the produce.

Continue east along the north side of Jermyn St, past the Jermyn Street Theatre (previously a restaurant but converted into a theatre in 1994), **turn left on Regent St and walk up the hill to Piccadilly Circus tube station, where the walk ends.**

River London

Start:	Westminster station
End:	Tower Hill tube station
Length:	3.5 miles (5.5 kilometres)
Time taken:	2 hours, plus stops in the many galleries and museums. A whole day can easily be spent on this walk
Eat and drink:	Lots of choices: Japanese restaurants in County Hall, cafés in the arts venues, many food stalls and restaurants around Borough Market, Dickens Inn at St Katharine Docks near the end of the walk
Includes:	Excellent river views along the entire walk, also County Hall, London Eye, Royal Festival Hall, National Theatre, Gabriel's Wharf, Oxo Tower and gallery, Bankside (art gallery), Tate Modern (art gallery), Shakespeare's Globe, Clink Prison Museum, Golden Hinde pirate ship replica, Borough Market, Southwark Cathedral, London Bridge Experience, London Dungeons, Britain at War Experience, Hays Galleria (former wharf converted to shopping centre), HMS Belfast (warship converted to museum), Tower Bridge, Tower Bridge Experience, St Katharine Docks, Tower of London

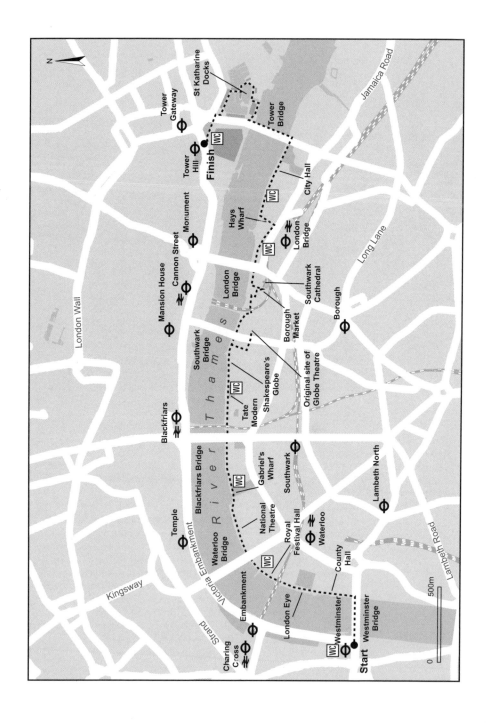

Best time: The river flows 24 hours a day, but Borough Market is only open on Thursday and Friday afternoons and all day Saturday. If you want to visit some of the attractions along the way, current opening times are: London Film Museum, London Eye, Bankside, Tate Modern, Shakespeare's Globe Theatre Exhibition and Tour, Clink Prison Museum, Golden Hind, 10 am - 5.30 most days, call 020 7403 0123; Borough Market, Thursday 11 am - 5 pm, Friday 12 - 6 pm; Saturday 8 am - 5 pm; Southwark Cathedral, Monday to Friday 8.30 am - 6 pm; London Bridge Experience, 10 am - 5 pm most days, call 0800 0434 666, pre-booking often required; London Dungeons, pre-booking often required, call 0207 403 7221 for information; Britain at War Experience, 10 am - 4.30 pm; HMS Belfast, 10 am - 5 pm; Tower Bridge Experience, 10 am - 5 pm; Tower of London, 10 am - 4.40 pm

Introduction

About 80 miles west of London, near the old Roman town of Cirencester, is an ordinary-looking field. The ground there is usually quite dry; only if there has been very heavy rain for the last few days can any water be seen there. Begin to walk east in the direction of London and a watercourse appears, which widens into a small river bed, usually still with no water in. In fact you may have to walk many miles downstream before you see any water flowing. From these small beginnings the Thames gradually grows, and by the time it reaches London it is a powerful river. As it heads further east it widens out into an estuary before finally reaching the North Sea.

During the Ice Age, when world water levels were lower, Britain was connected to the European mainland, and at that time the Thames flowed not into the sea but into what is now the Rhine in Germany. As temperatures warmed, the ice sheets melted and water levels rose, and the North Sea gradually separated Britain from mainland Europe. In fact this process still continues – the North Sea is attacking Britain from the east, and every year it eats away coastline. London itself is in such great danger of flooding that in 1982 the Thames Barrier was constructed in east London; it is a structure which can block the river completely when there is a risk of the North Sea flooding the city. It

was closed four times in the 1980s, 35 times in the 1990s, and 75 times between 2000 and 2010. For how much longer will the Thames Barrier be able to save London?

In the meantime, "Old Father Thames" is at the heart of London life, and has been for thousands of years. The modern river is cleaner today than it has been for centuries, and now supports swans, ducks, herons, crabs, otters and over 100 kinds of fish including salmon, eels and even seahorses It is clean enough to swim in, though dangerous in places and extremely cold. Leisure use of the river is now more common than commercial use, but there have been successful efforts in recent years to use the river as a means of transport because it is free of "traffic jams" and leads straight into the city centre. There is even serious talk of building a new airport for London at the mouth of the Thames and bringing travellers from there to the city centre on fast boats.

This walk takes you from Westminster to Tower Bridge, passing the most important river sites in historical and present-day London. Along the route are a great many arts venues, galleries and museums, some of them free. To visit all of them would take several days, so you may need to be selective in your choice of stops. Whether you stop or not, on this walk you can expect some world-class views of London's most famous buildings and bridges, and of course of the Thames itself.

Walk

Westminster Bridge

The Houses of Parliament, from across the river

Exit Westminster tube station and walk east across Westminster Bridge, from where you have an excellent view of the Houses of Parliament. Many artists have been inspired by the view of Parliament (or the Palace of Westminster which occupied the site before the current Parliament building was constructed), including Canaletto, Turner and Monet.

You should be able to see the two towers of Westminster Abbey sticking up behind the Houses of Parliament. The land on which these two iconic buildings stand was originally an island of relatively firm ground compared with the surrounding marshes (wet land). No island is visible today because of the embankments (walls) on both sides of the river, making it much narrower and faster-flowing than before their construction (see the walk Government London).

Walk north along the river bank to the enormous County Hall building.

County Hall

The curved section in the centre of County Hall was completed in 1922 and the north and south blocks added later in 1939. The building formerly housed the Greater London Council, the "parliament" of

County Hall, home to various restaurants and attractions

London, which during Margaret Thatcher's time as prime minister provocatively displayed anti-Thatcher flags on its front. The Iron Lady, watching from across the river in Parliament, was not amused, and her government closed down the Council in 1986.

On County Hall's ground floor are several Japanese restaurants (the building's owners are Japanese and have perhaps not yet learned to love British food) and an amusement arcade. The building also houses the London Film Museum, created as recently as 2008. It displays costumes and props (objects used by characters in films) from British productions, and has a section explaining how films are made. Also in County Hall is the Sea Life London Aquarium, the largest collection of marine life in the city.

Walk north from County Hall to Jubilee Park, where the London Eye towers above you.

London Eye

The London Eye is a statistician's dream. It is the tallest Ferris wheel in Europe at 135 metres, and the most popular paid tourist attraction in Britain with over 3.5 million visitors every year, making a total of more than 30 million so far. Its 32 capsules each weigh 10 tonnes and carry 25 people (or fewer, of course!). It turns at a speed of 26 cm per second, meaning that you have around 30 minutes to make small talk with your fellow-passengers.

In 2009 the Eye's capsules were

Thames Embankment

In the early nineteenth century much of London's sewage (toilet waste) went directly into the Thames; but the river was also the main source of drinking water for poorer Londoners, for whom the situation was a hygiene nightmare. The rich got their water from cleaner sources so were less affected; but no one could escape the filthy river's smell, which in the long hot summer of 1858 became unbearable to those near the Thames. In particular, politicians debating in Parliament, red-faced and hardly able to breathe, were forced to leave the building because of the "Great Stink", as it became known. Something had to be done - such an insult from the river could not be tolerated.

So, when the heat and the smell had gone and the nation's finest brains could once again focus, plans were put in place to deal properly with London's sewage. In 1875, thanks to the tireless work of engineer Joseph Bazalgette, a new sewage system was completed. Toilet waste continued to flow towards the river but now it was collected into a huge interceptor pipe inside the new embankment and "flushed" eastwards. Bazalgette's sewer network is still in use today, and every nose in Parliament is grateful.

The embankment created new land for London - about 50 football fields' worth - which was used for new parks. Tube lines were built into the embankment, and still run through it today.

The London Eye, a new icon for the capital

or search on YouTube for "London Eye fireworks mark new year 2011".

Continue east along the river bank. There are often street entertainers at this point. After you pass underneath Hungerford railway bridge, which has smaller footbridges on each side, look across to the park on the north side of the river. The buildings behind the park on its left side are about 150 metres from the river. As we know, before the Victoria Embankment was built the Thames was

improved, which involved taking them down one by one and floating them 25 miles down the river by barge to Tilbury Docks, then driving them 120 miles by lorry to the factory where they could be serviced. In order not to spoil the appearance of the Eye, replica capsules were temporarily hung in place of the missing ones.

Every year on New Year's Eve London hosts a spectacular fireworks display based around the London Eye. To see it, stay where you are until New Year's Eve,

Street entertainers along the South Bank

much wider, and it stretched nearly to where those buildings are.

The area where you now stand is known as a centre of culture, with a series of museums and arts venues along the river bank. Their architecture is not to everyone's taste, but they may be an improvement on the bombed-out buildings they replaced after World War II. **Continue to the Royal Festival Hall.**

Royal Festival Hall

Free entertainment most days at the Royal Festival Hall

The Royal Festival Hall was built for the 1951 Festival of Britain, like several other buildings on this walk. Inside it is a 2,900-seat concert hall, where the London Philharmonic Orchestra and Philharmonia Orchestra play the majority of their concerts. The theatre's foyer is always open to visitors, as are its restaurants and bars, most with excellent views over the river.

The foyer and bars of the Queen Elizabeth Hall, just east of the Royal

Youth culture is allowed to express itself under the Queen Elizabeth Hall

Festival Hall, are also open to visitors. More noticeable, though, is the building's colourful undercroft, famous for its graffiti artists, buskers (street musicians) and young skateboarders.

Behind the Queen Elizabeth Hall is the Hayward Gallery, which stages several major contemporary exhibitions a year, usually not free. BFI Southbank, Britain's leading cinema for classic film showings, is under Waterloo Bridge. It used to be known as the National Film Theatre, and the former name is still shown on the sign on the bridge. Under the bridge a book market often operates; when it is closed the books are stored in the wooden boxes beside the embankment wall.

After Waterloo Bridge, the next large building on the right is the National Theatre.

National Theatre

Arguments continue over the National Theatre's architecture

The National Theatre is a controversial creation in the brutalist style of architecture. If you immediately hate it you are in good company. Prince Charles remarked that the building was a clever way to build a power station in the middle of London without anyone complaining. On the other hand, the poet John Betjeman, who saved the Victorian masterpiece St Pancras Station from demolition (see the Transport London walk), described the National Theatre as "lovely" and "a great work". It has been voted into both the ten most popular and ten most hated buildings in Britain. The debate continues.

There are often outdoor performances in front of the theatre. Inside, the foyers are open to the public and contain a bookshop, restaurants, bars and often free exhibitions. There are usually free concerts in the main foyer, which is almost a theatre in itself, Monday to Saturday at 5.45 pm and on weekend days at 1 pm.

The Thames is tidal throughout London, and unless you do this walk extremely quickly you will probably notice a change in its level as you go. There is a seven-metre difference in the water level between low and high tides, and as you can see from the water marks on the river-side of the embankment walls, at high tide the water can rise to around 1 metre from the top.

London has sandy beaches where anyone can swim with a view of St Paul's Cathedral

If the tide is out, you will see a small sandy beach in front of the National Theatre. Who needs the Costa Del Sol? In fact the sand is not here naturally – it is dumped here for swimmers and anyone else who wants the use of a convenient urban beach. This may seem a strange idea today but it is not a new one. In the 1930s the authorities used to dump sand into the river by Tower Bridge to create a small city beach, which became known as the Cockney Riviera. It was just like a seaside beach, with entertainers, deck chairs, rowing boats for hire and as much swimming as you could manage, and tens of thousands of people took part.

When the tide is coming in, the Thames actually flows up-river (away from the sea), not downriver. There is usually enough rubbish floating on the river for you to see this clearly, but if not, you can test it yourself by throwing a stick or leaf into the river and watching it move surprisingly quickly. Over the centuries this characteristic of the river has proved helpful to invaders arriving via the North Sea, who simply waited till the tide was right and then drifted easily up the river.

Somerset House

Somerset House in its commanding riverside location

On the opposite side of the river from the National Theatre is Somerset House. In former days the north bank of the Thames at this point was lined with aristocratic mansions, of which little trace now remains except for streets named after the parts of England from where the buildings' owners came. For example, Northumberland Avenue is named after Northumberland House, London residence of the Duke of Northumberland. The magnificent Somerset House is in fact a rebuilding of an earlier palace of the same name.

A little way further east on the south bank, look for the viewpoint marker, a silver-coloured sign which maps the sights on the far side of the river. There are more such markers as you walk along the river bank.

Continue east to Gabriel's Wharf.

Gabriel's Wharf

Gabriel's Wharf is a collection of arty stalls and shops mostly selling craft products. Most of the shop-owners are also the designers and makers of the products they sell, and many are happy to do special commissions.

Outdoor café at Gabriel's Wharf

The land here was derelict (empty and unused) until 1988 when a local community organisation redeveloped it. The painted building on the west side of the shops is a former brewery, now part of a television studio complex.

River-side of the wharf is another small sandy river-beach where at low tide exotic sculptures are made from the sand. If you take a photograph the sculptors expect you to throw a coin or two to support their efforts. Children's sandcastle-building competitions are also sometimes held here.

Walk a little further east to the Oxo Tower.

Oxo Tower

The Oxo Tower is identifiable from the letters OXO near the top. Originally built as a power station, it was bought in the 1920s by a meat company and converted into a refrigeration building. One of the company's most popular products was Oxo stock cubes (beef flavouring), and they asked permission to advertise the product on the building's tower. Permission was refused, but the company put a circle, a cross and a circle on the tower and called it a "design", not an advertisement.

The tower's ground floor houses an art gallery with free exhibitions which you are welcome to visit. A fine balcony view can be had from the Oxo Tower's luxurious

Good views from the restaurant on the top floor the Oxo Tower

restaurant, brasserie and bar situated on the top floor, where a cup of tea will cost around £3, though no one can stop you from finding a table, enjoying the view for a minute and then "changing your mind".

Walk east to Blackfriars Bridge, where looking across the river to the north you will see the curved white frontage of Unilever House.

Unilever House

Unilever House was built in 1929 by Lord Leverhulme as the London headquarters of his soap company, which in 1930 became Unilever, makers of many cosmetic and cleaning products. We will resist the temptation to remark that in tests, nine out of ten customers said that Unilever House was much whiter than ordinary buildings.

Blackfriars Bridge itself is an attractive red-painted construction that was opened in 1869 by Queen Victoria, earning her a statue of herself by the bridge's north end. The west side of the bridge is decorated

Curved frontage of Unilever House at Blackfriars Bridge

with freshwater birds and the east side with sea birds and sea animals.

Just east of Blackfriars Bridge are the two rows of pillars that supported the former Blackfriars Railway Bridge, built in 1864. It became too weak to carry more modern trains, and the newer bridge you see to its east was built in 1886. At the southern end of the old bridge is the original abutment (a structure that supports a bridge), a highly decorated Victorian creation displaying the words London Chatham and Dover Railway.

Blackfriars Station, at the north end of the new bridge, is at the limits of its capacity and is being extended all the way along the bridge to the south bank of the

The new Blackfriars Railway Bridge under construction

Thames, where the station will have a new entrance. The present bridge will be widened to include at least one of the two rows of pillars from the old bridge – how fortunate that they were never removed. Solar panels on the new structure's roof will provide 50% of the station's electricity. When the new station is open, if you find this walk – or indeed Britain itself – too unexotic for your tastes you will be able on impulse to catch a train from here direct to Luton or Gatwick Airport, or to St Pancras International train station.

To see a video of the construction of the new Blackfriars Bridge, showing how some of the work was actually done from barges on the river, search on YouTube for "Blackfriars Station and Bridge Construction Works".

From here walk east to the Bankside Gallery.

Bankside Gallery and the Tate Modern

Small Bankside Gallery on the river front

The Bankside is a free-to-visit art gallery specialising in watercolours and prints. It is part of the Own Art scheme, which tries to make art affordable to everyone. The scheme applies to pieces of art priced at between £100 and £2000; instead of paying the full cost when you buy you can spread the payments over ten months with no extra charges.

50 metres east of the Bankside is the Tate Modern, another former power station. The Tate Modern is now the most popular modern art gallery in the world with 4.7 million visitors every year, and has the great benefit of being free to enter.

The Tate Modern art gallery building, a former power station

Just inside the main entrance is the five-storey-high Turbine Hall which features bespoke exhibits. Other parts of the building specialise in surrealist, cubist and abstract art, plus many other non-traditional styles.

Near the top of the Tate's chimney tower live two peregrine falcons, rare birds that are adapting to life in cities and developing a taste for pigeon meat. Peregrine falcons are the fastest creatures on earth, reaching speeds of over 200 miles per hour (325 kph) during dives. We can only pity any art-loving pigeon who flies Tate-wards when the peregrines are at home.

The bridge crossing the Thames to St Paul's Cathedral is the Millennium Bridge, or the "wobbly bridge", as many Londoners call it. When it opened in 2000 it was discovered that if large numbers of people shook the bridge at the same time they could make it wobble (move from side to side). Naturally, as soon as the authorities found out how exciting and popular the bridge had become, they closed it for two years while the "problem" was fixed.

To see a short film of the bridge wobbling, search on YouTube for "millennium bridge mdepablo".

Walk east to Cardinal's Wharf, a row of seventeenth-century houses that unlike most south bank buildings were not knocked down after World War II. On one of the houses is a plaque informing us that Christopher Wren, architect of St Paul's Cathedral and much else in London, stayed there, a statement that is almost

The Millennium Bridge, pointing the way to St Paul's Cathedral

Houses on Cardinal's Wharf

certainly untrue but which saved the house from destruction when the south bank was being redeveloped.

Continue east to Shakespeare's Globe.

Shakespeare's Globe

If your selection of this book means you have an interest in great literature, you will not want to miss the Globe, a reproduction of the seventeenth-century theatre of which William Shakespeare was a part-owner, and where some of his plays were performed. It was closed by the Puritans in 1642 and demolished two years later.

The man behind the recreation of the Globe was San Wanamaker, an American actor who was blacklisted (prevented from working because of his left-wing political views) in Hollywood in the 1950s so decided to move to Britain, where he

Shakespeare's Globe - a rebuilding of the seventeenth-century original

continued his acting and directing career. Dissatisfied that the original Globe was at that time commemorated only by a single dirty sign, in 1970 he founded the Shakespeare Globe Trust with the aim of building a replica of the theatre. He found money from private sources, notably the wealthy American businessman Samuel H Scripps, and also devoted much of his own income to the project. The difficulty of raising the millions of pounds that were necessary was however nothing compared with the endless bureaucratic problems. According to the New York Times the local council was "hostile" (negative and unfriendly) and even Wanamaker's colleagues were "skeptical".

He persisted, however, and in the 1990s rebuilding was finally able to begin. Wanamaker wanted the new theatre to be as close a replica of the original as possible, and, just in time, the remains of the old Globe were discovered nearby, ensuring the new theatre could be the same size as the original. The new building finally opened in 1997, four years after Sam Wanamaker's death.

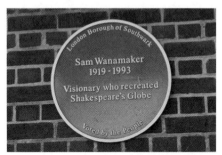

San Wanamaker, the man behind the rebuilding project

Performances at the Globe today are as authentic as possible: no microphones or lights are permitted, and only musical instruments from the correct historical period may be used. As in Shakespeare's time, much of the audience has to stand.

Like the modern-day Globe, the original stood on the bank of the river, but because the Thames was so much wider at that time the remains of the original are now around 100 metres south from here.

If you would like to make a short detour to see the site, directions will be given when we reach the Ferryman's Seat (see map).

Walk east along the bank and turn right into Bear Gardens, where on the left you will see a small stone set into the wall of a restaurant. A sign explains the stone was used by ferrymen to rest on while they waited for customers. London's bridges and roads were often crowded, and to be rowed across or along the river in a small boat was often the quickest way of travelling.

To see the remains of the original Globe Theatre, which will add about 10 minutes to the walk, go south on Bear Gardens to Park St, then turn left and go east under the bridge until you see the site on your right. As the signs explain, the remains are actually below ground level but are visible beneath glass.

The site of the original Globe Theatre

Follow your footsteps back to the river.

Walk east to Southwark Bridge (the pronunciation is "SU-therk"). In the passageway underneath it is a series of stones engraved with a poem about London's "frost fairs", which used to take place on the Thames when the surface froze completely during winter. This no longer happens for several reasons: winters are warmer nowadays; the embankments mean the Thames is narrower and therefore it flows faster, preventing freezing; and the newest London Bridge has wider arches, again allowing a faster flow of water.

Walbrook Wharf

Walbrook Wharf, where rubbish is transferred to barges and shipped down-river

Continue east. Just before Cannon Street Railway Bridge, look across to the north bank of the river and you will see Walbrook Wharf with its large black crane. 15% of London's waste is removed from the city by river barge, saving 100,000 truck journeys per year, and this is one of several places where rubbish is collected, put into yellow containers and lifted onto barges. The waste is then taken downriver to Kent, where it is sorted. The metal is recycled; all the rest is burnt, and the ashes are used to make bricks which in a neat life cycle are returned to London and used for building.

To see a 1-minute film of a rubbish barge on the Thames, search on YouTube for "Thames Tug towing rubbish barges London on 9th October 2010".

At Cannon Street Railway Bridge the path goes south a short way before continuing east; for the next kilometre we do not walk beside the river. As you pass under the bridge you may be tempted by an alcoholic aroma in the air from a nearby restaurant that specialises in cooking with wine.

For the rest of the walk we leave the cultural and artistic venues behind and pass instead a succession of tourist-oriented museums. First is the Clink Prison Museum just east of the bridge, built on the site of a medieval prison.

A little further on is the one remaining wall of Winchester Palace, built in around 1136 as the London residence of the

The Clink Prison Museum

Bishop of Winchester. The reason this one wall survived is that it was sandwiched between other buildings for many years until they were redeveloped.

Opposite the remains of the palace is the Golden Hinde shop, the premier

shopping destination for London's pirates, offering swords, moustaches, hats, books and everything else a self-respecting pirate should have.

That was the Golden Hinde shop; **now walk east to the Golden Hinde ship, or rather its replica.** The original was a pirate ship captained by Sir Francis Drake that received royal support from Queen Elizabeth I. Her encouragement was repaid when Drake returned from his travels with enough stolen Spanish gold to pay the entire government debt with ease. 400 years later, the current Queen Elizabeth may wish she could solve today's debt crisis by sending the replica Golden Hinde to rob the Spanish, but sadly the ship is used for nothing more sinful than pirate-themed children's parties. Before that it appeared in several films, and, in case anyone asks you, has sailed a total of 140,000 miles.

The Golden Hinde (replica), popular with today's young pirates

From the ship, follow the path south-east to **Southwark Cathedral**, whose main structure was built between 1220 and

Surviving wall of Winchester Palace

Southwark Cathedral, free and open to all

became more like a modern farmer's market, with a wide range of stalls and produce, and was fashionable with well-off middle-class shoppers, who were constantly instructed by TV chefs to "just pop down to Borough Market early in the morning for some fresh garlic", as if that were possible for viewers in the north of Scotland. Now it is changing again, as traders have realised they can profit from the constant stream of passing tourists.

Crowds seeking fine food and drink at Borough Market

1420, making it the oldest Gothic church building in London. The church authorities claim the site has been used for religious purposes since 606, which when pronounced "six-oh-six" apparently causes tourists from countries with a shorter history than Britain's to assume it refers not to a year but to a time of day. The cathedral can be visited free of charge.

Walk to the immediate south-west of the cathedral to Borough Market.

Borough Market

Borough Market operates on Thursday and Friday afternoons and all day Saturday. Its buildings are mostly Victorian but its history goes back much further. Traders began selling on London Bridge possibly as long ago as 1014, but because they slowed down traffic they were moved onto the south bank of the river, then in 1755 they were moved again to this site. Until the early 2000s Borough was a traditional-style market specialising in fruit and vegetables, but as the area gentrified (became more fashionable) it

Tourists' needs are different from those of householders – they like to buy food they can eat immediately, not food which they have to cook – and the market traders are therefore increasingly changing from selling fresh ingredients to providing ready-to-eat meals and snacks.

Another recent trend is that the market has become more continental in recent years, with traders from all over Europe, giving the venue a new character. The market buildings can be crowded and prices high, but there is a wide range of attractively-presented and appetising food on sale, and the market is well worth a visit.

A restaurant on the north side of the market, The Banana Store (located in a former banana storage warehouse), will cook whatever meat you buy at Borough Market and serve it to you with vegetables and garnishing, for £15 per person, but check the conditions on their sign.

Visit Southwark Cathedral if you wish, then walk east along its north side.

Just before London Bridge is the Mudlark Pub. In the eighteenth and

The Mudlark Pub, named in memory of the small children who searched for valuables in the river mud

Mudlarks

In the 1930s the word "mudlark" was a word used to describe London children who used to shout to passers-by to throw coins into the Thames mud for them to pick up. Some historians say that mudlarks were also part of criminal gangs - a fight would be intentionally started on board a ship, and during the confusion the ship's cargo would be thrown over the side for the mudlarks to pick up and run away with.

nineteenth centuries a mudlark was a small child who searched the Thames mud for items that could be sold for enough money to keep him or her alive.

London Bridge

From the Mudlark pub, look east and you will see one of the arches of London Bridge. This bridge is in fact just the most recent of a long line of "London Bridges" on this site; the earliest was a temporary one created by the Romans probably in around the year 50, and they almost certainly built more after that.

The Romans abandoned Britain in about the year 400, after which Saxon bridges were built here. In 1209 it was the Normans' turn – King John financed a bridge by licensing houses and shops to be built on it. That bridge served London well for 600 wobble-free years, until increasing amounts of traffic became too much for it to handle.

Therefore a new London Bridge, known as the Rennie Bridge after its chief engineer, was built in 1831. Unfortunately it was not as strong as its predecessor, and its east side began to sink slowly. London councillors came up with the original idea of selling the bridge, and in 1968 American oil millionaire Robert P McCulloch bought it and transported it to Arizona in pieces, where it was carefully reconstructed as part of an English theme park. Some say that McCulloch thought he

You can still go mudlarking, hopefully for fun rather than financial necessity. At low tide, simply walk on the Thames mud and try your luck. You will certainly find animal bones, from animals butchered (killed for meat) many years ago; seashells are also common - the contents were eaten and the shells thrown into the river; and there are plenty of old clay pipes (used for smoking tobacco). However, you may also find items of historical interest: valuable old coins, jewellery, pottery, old toys, weapons, in fact anything at all could be hiding under the mud waiting to be discovered. If you

find anything significant you have to report it to the Museum of London.

To see an eight-minute BBC report about mudlarking in the Thames, Google "Thames mudlarks uncover London's lost history".

One arch of the famous London Bridge

was buying the much more impressive Tower Bridge, but this has been denied by all concerned. The arch you can see above the road today is one part of the Rennie bridge that was never taken to Arizona; instead it was incorporated into the current bridge, which opened in 1973, and is a rather unspectacular structure when you consider the amount of history it represents (see article "Why does London exist?".

Walk east under London Bridge, where you will see one of the entrances to the London Bridge Experience, a museum that tells the story of London Bridge but with a Halloween-esque flavour. In a very similar style is the London Dungeon further east on the right. The two museums have accused each other of trying to steal each other's customers. Continue east past the Britain at War Experience, a museum which attempts to recreate the spirit of London during World War II. **Just before the Christmas Shop on your left, walk into Hays Galleria and stop by the huge moving sculpture in the main shopping area.**

Hays Galleria

Hays Galleria is a shopping centre whose interest lies in the fact that it was formerly a "wharf", an area where ships could load and unload. The floor you are standing on was once water – ships used to sail in from the river and unload goods into the warehouses on both sides. In the 1980s

Hays Galleria, formerly a wharf, now a shopping centre

the gates at the entrance were closed permanently, the wharf was filled in, and the Victorian-style roof was built.

Walk to the north end of Hays Galleria and continue east along the river. Many of the river-front buildings here are clearly former warehouses and wharves. Pass the HMS Belfast, a warship now converted into a museum.

Pass on your right The Scoop, an amphitheatre used for shows and films,

City Hall, home of the London's city parliament

and then City Hall, home of the Greater London Authority, London's local government. There are attempts to rename the building London House; some people jokingly call it the Motorcycle Helmet.

Across the river there are now good views of the Tower of London, begun in 1066 and one of the oldest buildings in London.

Climb the steps ahead and walk north across Tower Bridge. Most people think its name comes from its two towers but in fact it is named after the Tower of London.

The Tower Bridge's unique two-tower design had a reason: the intention was

Looking north across the river to the Tower of London

Why does London exist, and why here?

In the year 43 the invading Roman Army landed on Britain's south coast. Over time they pushed the local Celtic tribes north to the Thames a little way east of where London now stands. The Celts escaped across the Thames to its north bank, and the Romans, with all their heavy equipment, were not easily able to follow. They therefore travelled west looking for a place where the river was narrow and shallow enough to be bridged, and the location where you are standing was the first suitable place. Historians believe the Romans constructed some sort of floating bridge, probably a long row of small boats positioned side by side, in around the year 50. A few years later they built a more permanent wooden bridge. The Thames today would simply wash a wooden bridge away, but in those pre-embankment times the river was much wider, as we know, so it was shallower and flowed more slowly.

There are several further reasons why the Romans were drawn to this location: on the north bank were two hills offering dry land where a defendable camp could be built; there was a great deal of clay in the soil that could be used for brick-making; two smaller rivers, the Fleet and the Walbrook, which flowed south into the Thames, could be used as convenient harbours; the river's tides offered free power for sailing up or down the river; and the location was far enough from the sea that an unexpected attack by invaders was impossible. All these factors led to the building of the Roman city of Londinium (the origin of the word is not known for certain). Other Roman cities such as Verulamium (today's St Albans) and Camulodunum (Colchester) did not have these advantages, and so Londoninium quickly became the undisputed capital of Roman Britain. Roman remains can still be seen in London today, including several sections of the original city's defensive walls, and parts of an amphitheatre and a temple.

The fact that the Thames was first bridgeable by the Romans at this location has influenced much about Britain's modern-day transport network. When the Romans had developed Londinium they built a pattern of roads that radiated out from the city towards the other main population centres of Britain, and 2,000 years later the same pattern can be seen in today's road network. Many modern roads are in fact built upon former Roman roads, for example today's A5 was once the Roman road known as Watling St, which is why it is so straight, as the Romans built all their roads. Even today's railway network has been influenced by the Roman road pattern, with its lines radiating out from London to the major cities.

Tower Bridge, one of London's most recognisable sights

that when the bridge's roads were raised to allow tall ships to pass, pedestrians (walkers) wanting to cross the river could take the lift up one tower, cross the high walkway to the other tower, then take the other lift down and continue on their journey without being delayed. The Victorian architects did not foresee that when a ship was passing under the bridge what pedestrians wanted to do was stand and watch the sight; so the walkways were used only rarely, even though they offer marvellous views of London. Today they are part of the Tower Bridge Exhibition.

At the north end of Tower Bridge, go down the steps on your left and walk under the bridge. On this spot, directly under the road which passes over the bridge, you can see Irongate Stairs, famous among people of Jewish descent in Britain as the place where many of their nineteenth-century ancestors stepped onto British soil for the first time. They were escaping violence in Eastern Europe, and had undergone a long and difficult journey by road and ship to reach safety in Britain. Most were poor and hungry,

and spoke no English, so a struggle still lay ahead of them. See the walk Market London in this book, which describes something of the nineteenth- and early twentieth-century Jewish community near this part of London.

Walk east to St Katharine Docks, and stand with the river on your right and the Tower Hotel on your left.

St Katharine Docks

We saw at the Hays Galleria the impressive results of a Victorian wharf being converted for modern use; here we will see how a bankrupt industrial pre-Victorian dock can be transformed into a beautiful visitor-friendly attraction.

If you ask Londoners today where they think the centre of their city is, they will probably say the West End, perhaps Leicester Square or Trafalgar Square. Relatively speaking, however, those areas are new. London was founded near where we are now, and for well over 1,000 years, its centre was here. That explains why there was a dock on this site possibly as early as 1125.

View over St Katharine Docks

The present St Katharine Docks were planned and built in 1828 for the loading and unloading of ships from Europe, the West Indies, Africa and China. Commercially the docks were never very successful because they were too small for larger ships, which used London's many other docks further downstream. St Katharine Docks were heavily bombed during World War II and never recovered, finally closing in 1968. Subsequently many of the warehouses were knocked down and replaced in the 1970s by apartments and commercial properties, and the docks themselves became a marina.

Walk east past the Tower Hotel to the marina's entrance, which is only around 15 metres wide. Ships of up to 1,000 tons could pass through, but by 1900 ships were often more than 7,000 tons and were far too large for St Katharine Docks. **Walk north 50 metres, then walk east across the small bridge towards the curved white frontage of Devon House**, formerly occupied by the Port of London Authority.

Just east of Devon House is the Dickens Inn, an eighteenth-century brewery building now used as a restaurant. On Fridays a small food market takes place in this square.

Walk north over the small footbridge between two docks, then follow the path west. When you reach Nauticalia, makers

Devon House, overlooking small boats in the dock

and sellers of replica shipping memorabilia, turn right and walk north to the third and final dock. Continue to its north-east corner, then turn left and walk out of the docks via the north-west corner. Then follow the signs to Tower Bridge tube station, where the walk ends.

Theatre London

Start and end:	Covent Garden tube station
Length:	2 miles (3.25 kilometres)
Time taken:	1.5 hours plus shopping time
Eat and drink:	There are hundreds of options of all kinds in the streets around Covent Garden tube station and the Seven Dials area. Neal's Yard has some interesting vegetarian restaurants
Includes:	Donmar Warehouse, Neal's Yard ("new age" shops), Seven Dials, Cambridge Theatre, Earlham Street Market, Angels Fancy Dress shop, Tristan Bates Theatre, Ambassadors Theatre, St Martin's Theatre, The Ivy Restaurant, Screen Face (theatre make-up shop), Dress Circle (theatre shop), The Cinema Store, Garrick Club, St Paul's (the Actors' Church), Covent Garden Market, Adelphi Theatre, Nell Gwynne Tavern, Vaudeville Theatre, Savoy Theatre, Lyceum Theatre, Duchess Theatre, Novello Theatre, Aldwych Theatre, Brodie & Middleton (theatrical paint shop), Fortune Theatre, Theatre Royal Drury Lane, Royal Opera House, Royal Ballet School
Best time:	Any, but best during shopping hours

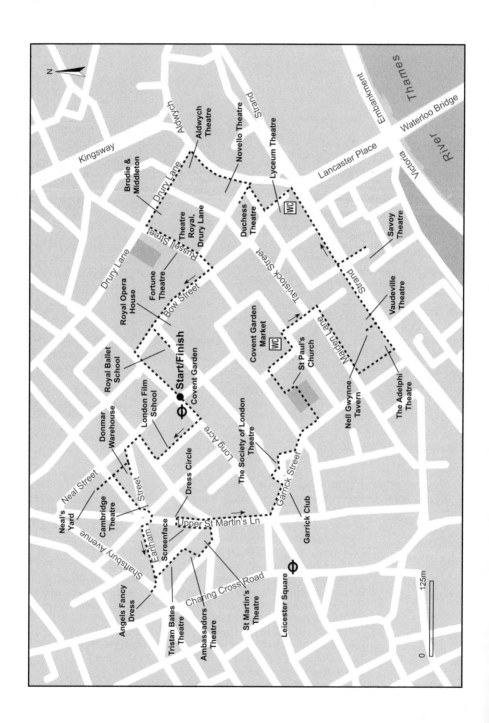

Introduction

With more than 50 major world-class theatres and many smaller venues, London is well known as the theatre capital of the world, with New York as its only real competitor.

There is a long tradition of theatre and night life in the Covent Garden district. Located away from London's business and government centres, it was far enough from official attention to be a suitable place for noisy drinking-houses. It also had plenty of dark alleyways for what we will tactfully call temporary commercial romances. These useful characteristics gave the area a reputation as a centre of entertainment, which eventually led to the building of theatres.

In the late twentieth century, increasing numbers of overseas visitors to London began to provide a huge new market for the city's theatres. Modern musical shows such as those of Andrew Lloyd Webber have been especially successful at attracting tourists. More serious plays are however still common in London, and in recent years have featured major stars like Nicole Kidman, Jude Law, Gwyneth Paltrow, Madonna, Jerry Hall, Matthew Perry, Christian Slater, James Earl Jones and others.

This walk covers the main locations in London's lively theatreland, including theatrical shops and businesses, St Paul's "the actors' church", The Ivy restaurant which is a favourite of theatre and film stars, the theatres themselves and other interesting sights such as the world-famous Covent Garden Market. Along the way there are plenty of shopping and eating opportunities and information about half-price theatre tickets.

Walk

London Film School

From Covent Garden underground station walk south-west on Long Acre and take the first right into Langley Street. A little way up the road on your right is the London Film School, founded in 1956. Its Chairman is Mike Leigh, a graduate of the school and director of realist British films such as Secrets and

Actors waiting to audition at the London Film School

Lies. Notice the school's cartoon-esque logo on its sign.

At the end of Langley St turn right into Shelton St and continue to a small square, then turn left into Earlham St and continue to the Donmar Warehouse on your right.

Donmar Warehouse

The Donmar Warehouse is a former brewery that became first a ballet rehearsal space then a theatre. In the 1990s its artistic director was Sam Mendes, who later directed several Hollywood films including *American Beauty* and *Jarhead*. Actors who have appeared at the Donmar include Ewan McGregor, Gwyneth Paltrow, and, perhaps most notably, Nicole Kidman, who appeared nude in *The Blue Room*. Sadly you have missed that performance, but at least you can see the building where it took place.

As with most theatres on this walk you can enter the foyer (reception area)

Donmar Warehouse, where Nicole Kidman appeared in The Blue Room

of the Donmar, from where if you wish you can exit directly into Thomas Neal's, an upmarket shopping centre whose shape is triangular because of the street layout caused by Seven Dials roundabout (see map). **Otherwise walk back east along Earlham St and then turn north into Cucumber Alley. When you reach Shorts Gardens you will see in front of you the entrance to Neal's Yard.**

Neal's Yard

Named (almost correctly) after seventeenth-century politician and property developer Thomas Neale, Neal's Yard features a back-rub centre, several cafes and various other "new age" shops.

The yard is the original location of the company Neal's Yard Remedies, which has grown from the small shop on this site into an international brand with stores in the USA and Japan.

Return to Shorts Gardens and walk south-west, passing on your right Neal's

Yard Dairy, a small grocery specialising in cheese, as your nose will tell you when you are some distance from the shop.

At the south-western end of Shorts Gardens, the last building on your right is the pub The Crown. Just to the right of its front door is a plaque explaining how to tell the time of day using the sundials you are about to see.

Neal's Yard, a little "new age" corner of London

British produce on sale at Neal's Yard Dairy

Seven Dials

Seven Dials is an open space with seven streets leading off it, but it has given its name to the whole surrounding area. In the centre of the square is a pillar with not seven but six sundials, not because the developers miscounted but because the original design was for six roads off the square.

The site was originally developed by the Thomas Neale referred to a moment ago. During the Victorian era Seven Dials became a dangerous slum, and in 1929 it was the sinister setting for Agatha Christie's Gothic detective novel *The Mystery of the Seven Dials*. Times have changed – today the only mystery is how Seven Dials has become one of the most fashionable shopping areas in London, its stores aimed mostly at young people.

Pillar at the centre of Seven Dials

Cambridge Theatre on the Seven Dials roundabout

Cambridge Theatre

On the south-eastern corner of the "square" (it is round) is the Cambridge Theatre, built in 1930 in a simple German-influenced style as a reaction against the highly decorative theatres of Victorian times. You can usually enter the two foyers, which are decorated with marble uplighters, concealed lighting and nude figures (it is beginning to look as though nudity and theatre are inseparable).

Recent productions staged: *Grease, Fame, Chicago*

From Seven Dials walk west along Earlham St, where a street market takes place every day except Sunday, specialising in flowers and second-hand clothes. When Earlham St bends to the right, look north across Shaftesbury Avenue and you will see the costume and fancy dress shop Angels.

Angels

Angels was founded by Morris Angel in 1840 as a small tailoring business. His shop soon became popular with actors from nearby Covent Garden, who in those days had to provide their own costumes. When they began to ask if they could hire costumes instead of buying them, Morris Angel saw the opportunity and started Angels' costume rental business.

By the 1920s the business was dressing many leading actors in Covent Garden. It also produced replacement costumes for Madame Tussaud's waxworks after they were destroyed in a fire (presumably a very long-lasting fire because of the main material involved). It then began providing costumes for films, starting with *Maid of the Mountains* in 1913 and followed by many more including *Lawrence of Arabia, Star Wars, Titanic* and *Elizabeth: the*

Angels fancy dress shop

home to the Actors' Centre, a venue for actors to experiment and develop new techniques and ideas. Past members include Judi Dench and Ian McKellan. There are often young actors and actresses entering or leaving the building, and you might find it interesting to ask one of them about the demands of their chosen profession. They will probably tell you that the life of an actor in London is difficult and uncertain. Although performers' wages are low, the competition for roles is fierce and professional actors can expect to spend long periods without work.

The Tristan Bates Theatre and Actors' Centre

Golden Age. During World War II the business supplied clothes to the Free French Army (uniforms, not fancy dress).

The Angels shop in Shaftesbury Avenue offers cheap fancy dress clothing for parties, and you are welcome to visit it and view the range of costumes. The business also has a warehouse in North London which holds more than a million costumes and supplies film, theatre and TV companies all around the world. The business is still owned by the Angel family.

The company has won many "Best Costume" Oscars. In 2008 it was the costume provider for all five Oscar nominations in the "Best Achievement in Costume" category.

Enter Tower St, where on your right you will see the Tristan Bates Theatre and The Actors' Centre.

Tristan Bates Theatre, The Actors' Centre

The Tristan Bates Theatre was founded by actor Alan Bates, who appeared in the films *Zorba the Greek* and *Spartacus*, and is named after his son who died aged just 19. It stages many innovative productions throughout the year. The building is also

Walk south-east down Tower St. When you reach Tower Court, with several Victorian shop-fronts on the left, turn right and walk to West St where you will see the Ambassadors and St Martin's Theatres.

Ambassadors Theatre and St Martin's Theatre

The Ambassadors and St Martin's were built as a pair by William Sprague, architect of a great many theatres and music-halls around Britain. Construction began in 1913 but was interrupted for several years by World War I. *Gone With The Wind* actress Vivien Leigh got her first major theatrical part at the Ambassadors in 1935, starring in *The Mask of Virtue*. In the audience was legendary British actor Laurence Olivier, who must have liked what he saw, because he and Vivien Leigh

it is still privately owned by his descendants. The theatre has a very attractive original foyer, visible through the window if the building is closed. Today the theatre is most famous as the home of Agatha Christie's play *The Mousetrap*, the world's longest-running theatrical production; its 24,000 performances so far have been watched by over 10 million theatre-goers. 382 actors and actresses (including Richard Attenborough) have featured in the play since 1952, and some have played the same role thousands of times.

Oh, and by the way, the murderer is... well, we must not spoil it for you.

The Ivy

Directly opposite the two theatres is The Ivy restaurant, whose very ordinary appearance contrasts with its reputation as a favourite spot of film and theatre stars. It opened in 1916 as an Italian café but its location in the heart of London's theatre district made it the perfect eatery of choice for showbusiness stars, and pre-war diners included Laurence Olivier, Marlene Dietrich, Dame Nellie Melba and Noël Coward. More recently, a patient observer outside the restaurant might have spotted stars like Tom Cruise, Brad Pitt, Jack Nicholson and Nicole Kidman, hopefully this time conforming to the restaurant's dress code.

The Ambassadors Theatre

began an affair, although both already had spouses. They finally married each other in 1940, but in true artistic tradition it was a stormy and difficult relationship full of extra-marital affairs, depression and illness.

The St Martin's Theatre was built in 1916 by Richard Greville Verney, an aristocrat with an interest in theatre, and

The Ivy, eating-place of the stars

The restaurant's windows are blocked out in order to prevent paparazzi from taking photographs of diners; but of course the easy way to see who is inside is to dine at the restaurant. Cameras and mobile

The Mousetrap - *still playing at the St Martin's Theatre since 1952*

phones are banned, so if you do meet any stars your friends will just have to take your word for it. It is difficult to get a table at The Ivy during normal dining times but you may have more luck at 5 pm or 11 pm.

Walk south-east then east to Monmouth St, then turn left and walk north up the hill to Screenface at no. 48.

Screenface

Screenface has specialised in theatre and film make-up for over 25 years; its products have been used in the Indiana Jones, Harry Potter and Monty Python films, and many more. Items on sale include wigs, fake eyebrows and beards, and artificial dirt, spiderwebs and blood (apparently ketchup is not used). The shop is happy to do your make-up for you.

Dress Circle - the world's oldest theatrical shop

globe turning on the roof of the Coliseum Theatre, home of English National Opera.

Walk south-east to Garrick St and continue to no. 15 on your right, the Garrick Club.

The Garrick Club

The Garrick is an exclusive club founded in 1831 for those involved in theatre and related fields, and is named after David

Screenface - for all your theatrical make-up

Cross the street and walk uphill a little further to The Dress Circle at no. 57.

The Dress Circle

The Dress Circle claims to be the world's oldest theatrical shop, in business since 1978. It sells a range of CDs, DVDs, sheet music, books, posters and other theatre-related merchandise such as Phantom of the Opera masks. In early 2011 the business was in financial difficulty and at risk of closure, but following well-publicised appearances at the store by performers such as Barry Manilow the shop's future seems more secure.

Walk south past The Cinema Store at Orion House on your right. When you reach the crossroads you can see downhill to the south a metal and glass

The Garrick Club - stars only, please

Garrick, a famous eighteenth-century actor much in demand by the fashionable aristocracy. Although women guests are admitted to many parts of the building, like many other London clubs the Garrick is men-only, a policy that has come under legal challenge.

It is difficult to become a member of the club, the original reason being that it was necessary to stop boring people from joining! Applicants can expect to wait many years for approval. The star-studded membership list has included Richard Burton, Yehudi Menuhin and Alec Guinness, and, today, Stephen Fry, Mark Knopfler and Roger Moore.

Go north up Floral St then turn right into Rose St and follow it left then right to no. 32, an office building housing several theatre-related organisations including the Society of London Theatre.

The Society of London Theatre

The Society of London Theatre is an organisation for London theatres, and offers half-price theatre tickets for performances on the same day of purchase. Tickets cannot be bought here; they are only available by going in person to the TKTS booth in Leicester Square. Take care to find the official TKTS booth, not other ticket shops nearby that claim to sell half-price tickets.

Half-price theatre tickets are on sale at the TKTS booth in Leicester Square

Next door is the Lamb and Flag pub, thought to be the oldest pub in the area, dating from 1623. Its nickname used to be the Bucket of Blood because of the bare-fist boxing fights once held here.

Walk downhill back onto Garrick St and turn left, then at the crossroads continue downhill into Bedford St to Inigo Place on the left. Turn here and you will see St Paul's Church.

St Paul's, Covent Garden (The Actors' Church)

Churchyard of St Paul's Covent Garden - "the actors' church"

St Paul's is a baroque church built by architect Inigo Jones in 1633. Its financier, the Earl of Bedford, was keen to keep construction costs low so he instructed the architect simply to build a "barn" (farm building). Jones promised to build him "the finest barn in Europe" – and he did. The church's garden graveyard is a quiet oasis in this busy area of London.

The church has associations with the acting community that date back to 1663, hence its nickname. On both sides of the path are benches mostly dedicated by theatre-related people and organisations. If the church is open when you visit, you will see inside memorials to many famous showbusiness names of recent years including Charlie Chaplin, Boris Karloff and Vivien Leigh, whom you may not be aware were all English.

Leave the churchyard via either the north or south side of the church and walk east to Covent Garden Piazza. Stand by the eastern wall of the church.

Covent Garden Piazza

Unconnected with the theatre but impossible to ignore, the busy Covent Garden Piazza has become world-famous. The land where it stands has fulfilled a

The Covent Garden Piazza, with the former fruit and vegetable market at its centre

variety of functions through the years: fields, Saxon town, fields again, then orchard, until the seventeenth century when it was developed into a fashionable Italianate-style square. Around 1654 there appeared on its south side a small fruit and vegetable market which step by gradual step became London's main wholesale grocery market, occupying the building you see today in the centre of the square. The father of film director Alfred Hitchcock ran a greengrocery business here. The market started very early in the morning, and often people coming out of the area's theatres late at night would see the first horse-drawn vegetable carts arriving from the countryside.

In the 1970s traffic problems forced the market to relocate out of central London, and the buildings became a shopping destination aimed mainly at tourists. The square is well known for its street performers, who are specially selected by the area's owners.

Standing by the church on the west side of the square you can still see signs of the building's past as a grocery market, such as the handcarts formerly used to move fruit and vegetables, the ramps used to get the handcarts into the buildings, and the trapdoors set into the ground. If you walk to the north side of the building you can see an old board with a long list of rules for the fruit and vegetable market.

Feel free to wander around the market before leaving the square via its south side and entering Southampton St. At no. 27 Southampton St on the right is the former house of David Garrick, mentioned previously in connection with the Garrick Club. **Continue downhill and turn right into Maiden Lane.**

Maiden Lane

As you walk west along Maiden Lane, notice on the left the many narrow passages leading downhill to the Strand. These are the alleyways referred to in the introduction to this walk, whose suitability for physical pleasures was one of the reasons why Covent Garden became London's main entertainment district.

Looking west down Maiden Lane

At no. 35 on the right is Rules, founded in 1798 and London's oldest restaurant. It has its own farm in the Pennine hills where it gets its meat. **A short distance further west on the left side is the back of the Adelphi Theatre.**

Adelphi Theatre

At the back of the Adelphi in Maiden Lane is a plaque commemorating the actor William Terriss, who in 1897 was murdered by Richard Arthur Prince, a colleague with whom he had argued. Prince escaped the death penalty, provoking London's theatrical community to accuse

the authorities of not viewing the murder of an actor as a serious crime! The angry ghost of Terriss is said to haunt the Adelphi to this day.

Continue west to the next alleyway just before the La Tasca restaurant, and follow it downhill to the Strand, then turn left and walk east to the front of the Adelphi Theatre at no. 409.

The present Adelphi is an Art Deco creation of the 1930s but the original theatre on this site was the Sans Pareil, built in 1806 by a father and his daughter – she wrote over 50 plays for the venue. Many works by Charles Dickens were adapted for the stage and performed at the Adelphi. The theatre also became known for its productions of sensationalistic melodramas nicknamed Adelphi Screamers.

In 1993 Andrew Lloyd Webber's company, the Really Useful Group, bought the theatre and refurbished it for his production of Sunset Boulevard. The film version of his musical Cats was shot at the Adelphi. To see a clip from the film, search on YouTube for "The Cats at the Jellicle Ball".

1930s frontage of the Adelphi Theatre

Recent productions staged: *Evita, The Jungle Book, My Fair Lady.*

Walk a short way east to a small alleyway called Bull Inn Court, where you may see a provocative sign.

Walk up Bull Inn Court to the Nell Gwynne Tavern.

Nell Gwynne Tavern

If the sign was provocative, it suits the former reputation of these alleyways and in fact of Nell Gwynne herself. See the mini-article on page xx, which describes her career as an actress and her relationship with King Charles II. **Then return to the Strand and walk east to the Vaudeville Theatre at no. 404.**

The Nell Gwynne Tavern, in an alleyway off the Strand

Vaudeville Theatre

Like most other London theatres the Vaudeville has been rebuilt several times on the same site, most recently in 1926. It still has rare nineteenth-century theatre equipment such as thunder drum and lightning sheets. It has hosted plays by JM Barrie, author of *Peter Pan*, and Jerome K Jerome, author of *Three Men in a Boat*. The most recent celebrity to appear at the theatre is Hollywood star Macauley Culkin in his first return to acting after a six-year break.

Like many other London theatres, the front of the Vaudeville is much narrower than the auditorium behind it. Space on a main road is expensive, so theatres are often built with small fronts that lead through corridors to a large auditorium set well back from the street.

The Vaudeville Theatre on the Strand

Recent productions staged: *Piaf, The Importance of Being Earnest, Stomp.*

Cross the Strand to the Savoy Theatre.

Savoy Theatre

The Savoy Theatre is located in Savoy Court, the only street in Britain where cars have to drive on the right. Beside it is the five-star Savoy Hotel.

The Savoy Theatre was built by impresario Richard D'Oyly Carte in 1881 as a venue for works by Gilbert and

The Art Deco entrance to the Savoy Theatre

Sullivan, Britain's most successful writers of light opera. It was the first theatre to have numbered seats (imagine the chaos before that!), and the first public building in the world to be lit by electricity. Gas, the previous method, had several disadvantages: it used oxygen and made the atmosphere difficult to breathe in, it caused too much heat, and it was a fire risk (many of the theatres mentioned in this walk have been damaged by fire in their history, some more than once).

The Savoy was expensively renovated in 1929, and like the Savoy Hotel is now considered an Art Deco masterpiece. It has played host to a great many famous names including the Pet Shop Boys and Simon Callow.

Cross to the north side of the Strand and walk east, then turn left into Wellington St where you will see the grand portico of the Lyceum Theatre.

The Lyceum Theatre

The Lyceum Theatre, host since 1999 to The Lion King

The Lyceum was founded in 1765, and though it began life as a theatre it has also served as a circus venue, the site of Madame Tussaud's first London waxworks display, a church, a concert room, a ballroom and a television broadcast studio. In the 1970s pop concerts were staged here by The Clash, Genesis, Bob Marley, Queen, The Police, The Who, U2 and many others.

Bram Stoker, author of *Dracula*, was business manager of the Lyceum for 20 years from 1878.

The story of Nell Gwynne and King Charles II

Nell Gwynne was born in 1650 in a Covent Garden alleyway and brought up by an alcoholic mother who owned a brothel. Despite that unlucky start in life, however, destiny had great plans for her. At the age of 13 the young Nell began work in a theatre as an orange-seller, but soon become an actress, and a very successful one.

For a young actress in those days, life was full of opportunity. It was common for an aristocrat to take a liking to an actress and keep her as a mistress on a handsome annual salary. Nell Gwynne cheerfully participated in this tradition, becoming associated first with actor Charles Hart and then the aristocrat Charles Sackville. However, it is for her relationship with a much more famous Charles that she is remembered. By 1668 it was well known in London that she was the mistress of King Charles II - or, as she joked, her Charles the Third.

Charles had a wife, Catherine of Braganza, but her pregnancies had all ended without a successful birth, and according to seventeenth-century royal politics this "failure" on her part reduced her influence and meant that Charles's mistresses had semi-official status. In 1670 Nell gave birth to the King's son. Controversially for a monarch's mistress, she continued to act in the theatre until retiring in 1671 aged 21, and in the same year gave birth to her second son by the King.

Charles had no children with his wife but he compensated for that by a producing a virtual football team outside of his marriage. His exact number of children is not clear but was perhaps between 12 and 17, by as many as eight different women. Despite the stiff competition, however, Nell Gwynne remained Charles' mistress until his death in 1685, far longer than anyone expected. You could say their seventeen-year relationship thus had a longer run than most other Covent Garden dramas.

Apparently Charles' deathbed words were: "Let not poor Nelly starve", and his brother and successor, King James II, obeyed, giving Nell a generous pension and a property which remained in her family until 1940.

There are interesting similarities between Nell's life and that of Eva Peron. Both were born outside of marriage into poverty, both became famous actresses, both progressed upwards through society via a series of affairs with ever more influential men, and both ultimately had a long-term relationship with the most powerful man in the country. Did Eva take inspiration from Nell, we ask excitedly? All we know for certain is that the musical *Evita*, based on Eva Peron's life, played at the Adelphi, only a few metres from where you are standing.

Amazingly, Nell Gwynne's influence survives today. According to a BBC report of 2006, "research suggests" Nell is the great-great-great-great-great-great-great-great-grandmother of Samantha Cameron, wife of Prime Minister David Cameron, who like her ancestor exerts her charms on the most powerful man in Britain of the time. Coincidence or genetics?

Since 1999 the theatre has hosted *The Lion King*, whose audience count now exceeds 8 million. Prime Minister David Cameron attended the show's tenth anniversary performance.

Recent productions staged: *Jesus Christ Superstar, Oklahoma!, Macbeth.*

Walk north to Exeter St and then turn right into Catherine St, then turn left and walk north to the Duchess Theatre on your left.

Duchess Theatre

The Duchess Theatre is one of the smaller West End theatres, seating just 479. Architecturally its most interesting feature is that its auditorium is set partly below ground level so that the entire building can be lower and thus avoid blocking light to neighbouring buildings.

The Duchess holds the record for the shortest ever West End run – in 1930 *The Intimate Revue* closed before even its first performance.

The Duchess Theatre just off the Strand

Go back downhill to the Aldwych, then walk north-east to the Novello and Aldwych Theatres.

Novello Theatre and Aldwych Theatre

The Novello and Aldwych theatres, on either side of the Waldorf Hotel, were also built as a pair by William Sprague in 1905.

The Novello Theatre has been renamed for Welsh musical composer, songwriter and actor Ivor Novello, who lived in a flat above the theatre for nearly 40 years.

The Aldwych Theatre is named after the curved street on which it stands. "Aldwych" means "old market town",

The Aldwych Theatre in a rustic setting

referring to the Saxon settlement of Lundenwic which in the seventh century covered most of what is now the Covent Garden district.

Recent productions staged: *Desperately Seeking Susan, Footloose, Buddy, Dirty Dancing, Fame, Dancing in the Streets.*

From the Aldwych walk north up Drury Lane to Brodie & Middleton at no. 68 on the left.

Brodie & Middleton

Brodie & Middleton have been supplying theatrical scenery paint and equipment to London's acting community since the 1840s. They still sell traditional-style products as well as a more modern selection. The range includes not just paint but also dyes, theatrical make-up and fabric for stage backgrounds. They also provide a range of materials for "distressing" costumes (making them look older).

Walk north to Russell St and turn left, then walk west to the Fortune Theatre on your right.

Fortune Theatre

The Fortune Theatre opened in 1924, the first to be built in London after World War I. On the theatre's facade is a figurine of

The Novello Theatre on the Aldwych

Terpsichore, one of the nine Muses in Greek mythology.

Judi Dench and Dirk Bogarde have both appeared at the Fortune. Since 1989 the theatre has staged the two-actor play *The Woman in Black*, now the second-longest-running production in London after *The Mousetrap*.

Theatre Royal

The "Theatre Royal, Drury Lane", to use its full and correctly-punctuated name, is the oldest theatre in London, dating back to 1663. The current building was constructed in 1812, the fourth on this site.

During a performance at the theatre in 1800 a mentally disturbed ex-soldier named James Hadfield tried to assassinate King George III, firing several gunshots and only narrowly missing his target. He was quickly brought under control, and the king calmly ordered the performance to continue.

The Theatre Royal has long been known for ambitious stage effects. The 1823 production of *Cataract of the Ganges* featured a horse racing up a flowing river surrounded by fire. In 1909 a play titled *The Whip* required twelve horses to race on stage. More recently, the musical *Miss Saigon* included the spectacle of a helicopter descending into the stage area.

In a supernatural sense the theatre is rather crowded because it is said to be haunted by an impressive total of four ghosts, among them that of celebrated English clown Joseph Grimaldi. Charmingly, his ghost is said to guide uncertain actors helpfully around the stage.

Theatre Royal, Drury Lane, haunted by several ghosts

It was in the Theatre Royal that Nell Gwynne worked as an orange-seller, as explained on a board outside the pub Nell of Old Drury opposite the theatre's entrance.

Recent productions staged: *South Pacific, The King and I, Shrek the Musical.*

Continue west along Russell St, turn north on Bow St and walk north to the Royal Opera House.

Royal Opera House

The Royal Opera House, said to be the most modern theatre complex in Europe

The Royal Opera House is home to the Royal Opera Company and the Royal Ballet. The structure was originally built in 1732 but has been reconstructed three times, most recently in 1992 after much expense and controversy. The complex, claimed to be the most modern in Europe, houses three performance spaces including the magnificent main auditorium dating from 1858. Two alternative guided tours are offered on most days, one of the backstage area (during which you may see ballet rehearsals) and another of the auditorium.

The foyer is usually open and usually features a theatre-related exhibition which you are welcome to visit.

Recent productions staged: *La Traviata, Swan Lake, Carmen.*

Just to the north of the Royal Opera House is Floral St. Go west along it to no. 50, where a plaque informs you that in this building Pablo Picasso painted the backdrop for *Le Tricorne*, a production by the Russian ballet company Ballets Russes.

Royal Ballet School

A little further west at no. 46 Floral St is the Royal Ballet School, associated with the Royal Ballet and one of the world's leading ballet schools.

If the life of a young actor in London is difficult, the life of a young ballet dancer is even more so. Competition is if anything more intense because, unlike acting, ballet-dancing does not require a good command of English, so is open to performers from the whole world. Actors do not necessarily need to start young or have any particular physical attributes, whereas professional ballet dancers usually start before the age of 10 and have to maintain top fitness throughout their working life. Unofficially, they also need to have the right body shape and be within a certain height range, criteria that would be illegal in any other job!

Moreover, whereas an actor can continue to work most of his life, it is unusual for a ballerina to dance beyond the age of 30, perhaps 35 for male dancers. In the top ballet companies an exhausting schedule of rehearsals is common, around seven or eight hours of dancing per day, and injuries are frequent. The work can also be emotionally draining because of the obsessively high standards demanded by major companies. There is some truth in the stereotype of a tyrannical female choreographer, grey-haired but still slim from her own dancing days, screaming Russian-accented abuse at an unfortunate young ballerina.

Return to Bow St and walk north, then turn left on Long Acre and continue to Covent Garden tube station, where the walk ends.

Ballet in London

Ballet originated in Italy in the 1400s as a dance version of fencing (safe fighting with swords for sport, as in the James Bond film *Die Another Day*. Search on YouTube for "Die Another Day - Fencing Scene Part 1 [HD].avi"). From Italy it spread to France, where in 1661 Louis XIV, himself a keen ballet dancer, set up a dance academy which attempted to set professional academic standards for ballet. It is because the art became formalised during this period that the terms used in ballet today are mostly French: pas de deux, grand jeté, arabesque, and hundreds of others.

Ballet fell out of fashion in France in the 1830s, but it continued in other countries including Italy, Denmark and especially Russia, where it reached new heights of popularity through the ballets of Tchaikovsky. It was the formation in Russia in 1909 of the Ballets Russes and their later international performances that reintroduced classical ballet to western Europe. One of the company's dancers was Irish-born Ninette de Valois, who in 1926 created the Royal Ballet School in London and thereby brought English ballet into being (which must have been a difficult task, in view of the well-known English dislike for learning even a few words of French).

Ninette de Valois was of the most influential figures in ballet in the twentieth century - literally, because she lived from 1898 till 2001. She retired from the Royal Ballet in 1963 but continued to make public appearances until her death at the age of 102.

The Royal Ballet School in Floral Street

Shopping London 2

Start:	Charing Cross tube station
End:	Tottenham Court Road tube station
Length:	1.5 miles
Time taken:	1 hour plus shopping time
Eat and drink:	This walk covers Chinatown with its many restaurants and cafés, but there are lots of other options along the way
Includes:	William Curley (chocolate shop), Cecil Court (London's former film district, now a second-hand book district), Chinatown, Shaolin Way (martial arts shop), Chinatown back alleys, New Loon Moon Supermarket, GuangHwa Chinese bookshop, Chinatown Market gift shop, G Smith & Sons (snuff shop), Foyle's bookshop, Denmark St (London's music street), Regent Sounds Studios (former recording studio of Ozzy Osborne, the Rolling Stones and others), former flat of the Sex Pistols, former workplace of Elton John where Your Song was written
Best time:	During shopping hours

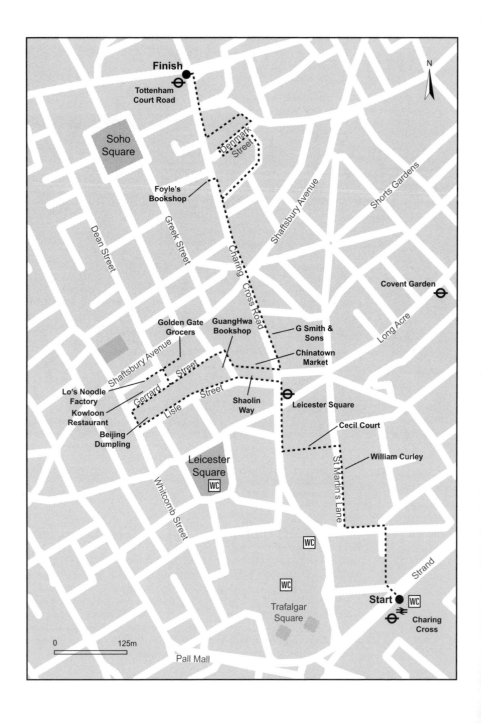

Introduction

If Shopping London 1 has not exhausted either your budget or your appetite for shopping, fear not – there are plenty more opportunities to shop – or window shop.

Shopping London 1 was concerned more with traditional-style English shops, but this walk has a wider focus. It takes us to London's book district, its Chinatown, its "music street", a tiny Koreatown, and various other shops of interest. The city's electronic shop district and furniture district are near the area covered and can be explored independently.

The title of this chapter does not mean that you need to do any shopping while on the walk. The aim here is simply to see some interesting shops with unusual products, and also to learn a little of the history behind some of London's shopping areas as you walk.

However, if you are in the mood for "retail therapy" there will be plenty of opportunities, to suit all budgets. The walk has been designed partly to take you to shops where you can make inexpensive but interesting "impulse" purchases if you like. Also, there will be a great many eating opportunities en route, especially in Chinatown. You can choose whether to stop somewhere and have a sit-down meal or to enjoy snacks as you go. Or – since your author wants you to enjoy yourself and is not paying your bills – why not both?

Walk

Exit Charing Cross Station via exit number 6 and walk up St Martin's Lane. Pass the Coliseum Theatre on your right, and shortly afterwards temptation will appear in the form of the shop William Curley, Patissier and Chocolatier. The two owners of the business are a (slim!) husband and wife team from Scotland who have three chocolate shops in rich London locations, all offering chocolates they themselves have designed.

You know you want to! We have prepared an excuse for you: the chocolates will give you energy for the walk.

Continue north to the Quaker Meeting

Freed of London and New York, makers of dance shoes and clothing

House on your right, then cross the road to its west side. On the corner of St Martin's Lane and Cecil Court is Freed, a specialist clothes shop for ballerinas (or for people who like to dress as ballerinas). As well as selling a wide range of ballet clothing and shoes, they also make bespoke shoes for professional dancers.

Enter Cecil Court, known today as a street of bookshops, and walk west.

When you reach Charing Cross Rd turn and walk north past no. 30, Gaby's Deli, once visited by Charlie Chaplin and now a favourite of theatre stars including Vanessa Redgrave and Blur's bass player Alex James. The 70-year-old owner, who opened his Jewish delicatessen business here in 1965, is fighting plans to close it and replace it with a restaurant.

Continue north to Leicester Sq tube station and cross to the west side of the road, then walk north to Little Newport St and under the street sign, which as you can see from its Chinese lettering is part of Chinatown.

Cecil Court

Around 100 years ago, however, in the very early days of silent film, this unglamorous passage was the Hollywood of Britain, known as Flicker Alley because of all its film-related businesses. Why here? Records are unclear but it may be because manufacturers of film equipment such as lenses, cameras and projectors were located nearby. Whatever the reason, all the major film studios had soon set up offices here, and among their neighbours were film distributors, equipment makers of various types and cinema builders.

The very word "flicker" (move unsteadily) tells us that the picture quality of films in those early years was far from perfect. By today's standards some of the films are barely watchable from an entertainment point of view but are fascinating in a historical context. To see an example, search on

Looking west down Cecil Court

YouTube for "Hepworth Alice", and you will find the first ever film version of *Alice in Wonderland*, released by British film pioneer Cecil Hepworth from 17 Cecil Court in 1903. Over 100 years later it is a charming little piece of Edwardian cinematic history, just 10 minutes long.

Cecil Court's starring role in British cinema was short-lived. As the film companies grew they needed bigger premises, and by 1914 most had moved to Wardour St in nearby Soho.

Today Britain has several major film studios including Shepperton (since 1931), Pinewood (since 1934, named as a reference to Hollywood), Teddington (since 1910), Elstree (since 1927), and, since 1902, Ealing Studios, the oldest film studios in continuous operation anywhere in the world. Soho, where many of the Cecil Court film companies moved nearly 100 years ago, is still home to many small TV and film companies such as The Mill, which won an Oscar for its work on *Gladiator*.

Reminders of Cecil Court's history of film-making

In 2007 an academic at Manchester University wrote an article about the history of Flicker Alley, which reawakened interest in Cecil Court's role in British cinema. Following that article, many shops in the street have stuck round blue signs in their windows listing the film-related businesses that once occupied the buildings

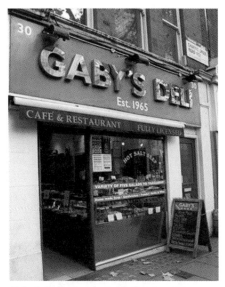

Gaby's Deli, popular with theatre stars

Little Newport St, Chinatown

London's Chinatown is a colourful and aromatic district of the city, popular with locals having a night out in the West End, tourists seeking a cheap Chinese meal, and with British Chinese, who use the street for specialist shopping and as a community focal point.

Look up at the street sign for Little Newport St – if you are still standing there! The English-language street name has four Chinese characters underneath: one for "little", one for "new", one for "port" and one for "street". That translation method is fine when the English word has a meaning but not when it is a name, such as "England". Chinese normally solves that

Chinatown Street names in English and Chinese

problem by using Chinese syllables (Chinese does not have an alphabet with letters) that sound similar to the English word; for example, "England" is pronounced "Ying-ger-lan".

There are two types of Chinese characters: the "original" ones used by around 30 million people in Hong Kong, Taiwan and overseas Chinese communities; and the simplified versions used by over 1.3 billion people in the People's Republic of China. Because most Chinatown residents originally came from Hong Kong, the traditional characters are used on Chinatown's signs, but perhaps not forever.

Walk west along Little Newport St. On the right at no. 10 is Shaolin Way, a martial arts equipment and clothing store named after the Shaolin Monastery in north-central China which was founded in the fifth century and is still famous for its martial monks.

Shaolin Way, supplier of Chinese martial arts equipment

Continue west along Lisle St. A short way along on the right at no. 23 is a restaurant called Beijing Dumpling where you can often see staff making Chinese dumplings by hand in the window. Note that the restaurant's name refers to "Beijing", perhaps a reference to mainland China's growing influence in Chinatown.

At the end of Lisle St turn right into Wardour St, and a short way north on the left is the restaurant Wong Kei, pronounced "Wonky's" by its fans. Your author has heard that its service is

Chinatown

There are hundreds of Chinatowns in the world, in all continents, and not all are like London's. They range from the large to the small, the lively to the near-dead, the fashionable to the forgotten, the wealthy to the poor, the industrial to the tourist-oriented. They appear for a variety of reasons. The first Chinatowns were small trading communities developed by rich Chinese traders in the late seventeenth century in Asian ports like Nagasaki, Manila and Hoi An in Vietnam, followed in the eighteenth century by Chinatowns in Bangkok and Jakarta.

In the nineteenth century thousands of Chinese hoping to escape poverty and the unstable political situation in China went to the USA to work in gold mines and, famously, to build the railways in the newly-opening western states. The USA's Chinese presence is still concentrated on the west coast, though most major American cities have a Chinatown. In the nineteenth century the opening of mines in Australia, New Zealand and South Africa also led to the establishment of Chinese communities in those countries.

European Chinatowns, such as those of Germany and the Netherlands, are of much more recent origin. The first Chinatown in London

Looking east along Gerrard St in Chinatown

started in Victorian times around the docks of Limehouse in East London, catering to the Chinese sailors who stayed there, often hoping to earn enough to buy a ticket back to China. A few traces of Chinese Limehouse remain: gravestones with Chinese names, several Chinese street names, a Chinese Sunday school and community centre, and one or two restaurants including Local Friends at 102 Salmon Lane, one of the oldest Chinese take-aways in Britain, founded in the 1950s. After World War II, during which Limehouse was heavily bombed, most Chinese moved to Soho, the site of today's Chinatown, which at that time was not the lively area it is now. Their timing was lucky because many British and American soldiers in London had learned to like Chinese food during their wartime service in the Far East, and the new residents of Soho were happy to set up restaurants to serve them.

During the 1950s and '60s the Chinese population in London was increased by a new wave of immigration from Hong Kong, then a British colony, with the result that many more restaurants appeared in Soho. By the late 1970s "Chinatown" had become a recognisable destination, and it continues to attract the crowds today.

famously "informal" – for example, there are stories of waiters standing behind your chair waiting for you to finish so they can quickly put the next person in your place. The restaurant is popular with students, who apparently see this sort of service as a kind of entertainment!

Wong Kei, student favourite and one of the largest Chinese restaurants in Britain

One of the original Chinatown businesses, dating from the 1960s

Gerrard St

Go south a few steps then turn east into Chinatown's main road, Gerrard St, with red gates called Paifang at each end. Paifang have been built in many Chinatowns worldwide, sometimes funded by the Chinese government and sometimes by local governments who believe they promote tourism.

Walk east along Gerrard St. At no. 21 on the left is the Kowloon Restaurant and Cake Shop, founded in 1969 and one of the original Chinatown businesses. Kowloon, meaning "nine dragons", is an area in Hong Kong.

A little further east on the south side of the street is a board with various notices about events including Chinese music classes and English lessons for Chinese people.

For an atmospheric glimpse of authentic back-street Chinatown, completely unknown to the tourists who pass by just metres away, turn left into Macclesfield St then left again into Dansey Place. You will feel as though you are in a scene from the film *Big Trouble in Little China* (search on YouTube for "Big Trouble In Little China (1986) Part 2" to understand what is meant by that). A short way along on the left is a Chinese fish shop with tanks full of lobsters, eels and other fishy delights. A little further on the left is a doorway leading up some stairs to Lo's Noodle Factory, which supplies many of the restaurants in Chinatown with noodles but welcomes passers-by with a hunger for fresh noodles or the business's other offerings, which include Chinese buns, dumplings and cake.

Walk back to Macclesfield St and cross it into Horse and Dolphin Yard, where there is a market stall selling cheap vegetables, many kinds of which you may not be familiar with, and the Golden Gate Grocers.

Go back to Gerrard St and continue east. At no. 9 on the left is the New Loon Moon Supermarket, which in a sign of the times is not a "Chinese" grocery but an "Asian" one, with products from not just China but also Korea, Japan, the Philippines and elsewhere. If you are not from Asia many of the shop's products will be new to you, so you may find it interesting to explore the shop and see the products on offer. YYou may never have seen Chinese food uncooked before! See the mini-article in this book for suggestions of snacks you can try.

After leaving the shop continue east along Gerrard St then enter Newport Place. At no. 7 is GuangHwa, which sells books, arts and crafts. There is a large section of English-language books

New Loon Moon Supermarket

The New Loon Moon is an excellent place to buy snacks. There is such a wide range of food on offer that it hard to know where to begin, but for a snack here and now you could ask the shop assistants on the ground floor to help you find coated green peas, coconut flavour coated peanuts, buco-pandan wafer stick, or shrimp peanut crackers. To wash your snack down you could try aloe vera drink, Wong Lo Kat herbal tea in cans, or grass jelly drink.

On the first floor ask for pandan rice cake, Japanese mochi, or dried fruit, of which there are many types including plums, mandarin orange, mango, star fruit, kumquat and sweet potato.

For something to eat later, or to give as a small present, downstairs there is a range of Chinese tea, also a large section for biscuits, and soaps including coconut oil and papaya.

Gift shop in Chinatown with lots of colourful products on sale

place to stock up on little gifts and items for a China-themed children's party. Upstairs is a Brazilian café and an enormous collection of children's stickers.

Charing Cross Road

Leave Chinatown Market and return to Charing Cross Rd, then cross to the east side of the road and walk north. On your right are several more bookshops, some selling collectors' items, others selling cheap second-hand books. At no. 68 is an apparently unnamed shop selling a variety of punk, goth and rock badges, bracelets and jewellery. No. 70 still has curved pieces of metal sticking out and down from its sign-board – these used to hold lights that shone on the shop's outdoor book displays.

At no. 74 is G Smith & Sons, which specialises in snuff, a form of crushed tobacco that is inserted into the nose

about China and materials for Chinese calligraphy.

Opposite GuangHwa is a business called Chinatown Market, which actually has three shops in the same building. To see the biggest and best, go east into Newport Court and find their doorway on the left.

The shop front looks small but the store opens up into an Aladdin's cave inside, with a range of cheap gifts such as model Buddhas, chopsticks, "jade" dragons, lanterns, tea sets, umbrellas, earrings, and a variety of other things. It is an ideal

Eccentric shop on Charing Cross Road

rather than smoked. Use of snuff has been documented ever since Europeans reached the Americas. In eighteenth-century Britain, the taking of snuff was popular among the upper classes, while the lower classes generally smoked. Snuff-taking was fast disappearing from Britain until the recent ban on indoor smoking (which is the reason why the shop has a "no smoking" sign on its door!); so snuff is now making a comeback, and there may be a bright future for G Smith & Sons. Snuff-taking is not as harmful to the health as tobacco smoking but it still carries risks.

Walk north across Cambridge Circus, with the Palace Theatre on its west side, then continue up Charing Cross Rd past Blackwell's, an academic book-selling company which began in Oxford in 1879. Cross to the west side of Charing Cross Rd when you see Foyle's, one of the largest bookshops in Britain, with 30 miles (50 kilometres) of shelves. From Foyle's,

One of Britain's few remaining snuff shops

Foyle's

Foyle's, one of the largest bookshops in Britain

The history of Foyle's is more eventful than you might expect of a bookshop. The business began in 1903 when brothers William and Gilbert Foyle successfully sold some of their old text books, which encouraged them to set up a bookshop from their home. The following year they opened a shop in Cecil Court during the heyday of the silent films. Their first assistant stole cash from the business and disappeared, but the brothers were luckier with their second one, who joined in 1905 and stayed for over 45 years. By 1906 more space was required and the business moved to Charing Cross Rd. Its van became a common sight on the streets of London as it drove around delivering books to customers. In those days it was possible to buy books by posting an order to the shop, and Foyle's would receive thousands of such orders every day.

In the 1930s Hitler began his campaign of burning books. William Foyle contacted the German government offering to buy the books at a good price, but received an unimpressed "Nein" in reply. When World War II broke out and bombing raids were taking place over London, Foyle's covered their store roof with copies of Mein Kampf to try to keep the bombers away. The strategy apparently worked - the store was never struck by a bomb.

By the year 2000 the business was in need of modernisation, so the whole five-storey building was given a makeover (smartened up) for the twenty-first century, and a web site was launched. Today the shop also hosts events such as classical music concerts and meetings with authors, usually free to attend.

Foyle's, post-makeover

Denmark St

Denmark St has been called Britain's "Tin Pan Alley", from the expression referring to West 28th St in New York, which from 1885 was the location of many music publishers. In those days if you wanted to listen to music at home you had to learn how to play an instrument yourself, and the publishers' role was to find new songs and turn them into printed sheet music for pianists and other musicians. Songwriters would go to the publishers' offices and play their songs on the piano, hoping to sell them.

There are at least two theories as to the origin of the nickname "Tin Pan Alley". The first relates to the New York Times, which reported that the chaotic noise in the street from so

Looking east along Denmark St, London's "music street"

many pianos being played at the same time sounded like tins and pans being banged in an alleyway. The second and much more likeable theory Is that as songwriters played their compositions for the publishers, less talented writers would listen from the streets and write down the tunes, hoping to sell them as their own. To prevent this dishonesty the songwriters paid people to stand in the street and bang a tin pan so that the music could not be properly heard. If only the music industry's piracy problems could be solved in that way today.

Around the mid-twentieth century the market for printed sheet music ended with the introduction of phonographs (record players) and radios, and the businesses in Tin Pan Alley closed down one by one.

The story of Denmark St starts the same but ends very differently. Its origins lie in the nineteenth century when its cheap rents made it a desirable living area for struggling composers and songwriters who needed to be near the theatres and music-halls of Covent Garden and the West End. In the 1890s music publishers began to move in, and by the 1930s a lively sheet music industry had developed. As a secondary business, some of the publishers started to display pianos and guitars for sale, a practice which grew and ultimately led to the musical instrument stores of today.

Technology may have caused the death of New York's Tin Pan Alley but it brought London's very much to life. It was in the 1960s, when recording studios opened here, that Denmark St started to become associated with recordings by artists like Jimi Hendrix, the Sex Pistols, the Rolling Stones and the Beatles. Eric Clapton, Pete Townshend and Bob Marley are thought to have bought guitars here. Many more music publishers set up shop in the street at that time, and it has been said that in the '60s you could sit in a Denmark St café and write a song, then walk into a music publisher's office and sell it immediately for £5.

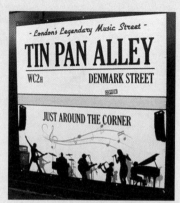

Denmark St, London's answer to New York's Tin Pan Alley

cross back to the east side of Charing Cross Rd and walk south a few steps, then turn left into Flitcroft St, walk east to the end then turn left and left again into Denmark St, London's "music street". Today it is home mostly to musical instrument shops, but in the 1960s these pavements were walked by many young musicians who are now world-famous pop stars.

Virtually every building in Denmark St is loaded with musical history. We will walk west along the south side of the road then back east along the north side.

Walk west to no. 4, where Regent Sounds Studio was established in the late 1950s originally to produce acetates (records) mostly of jazz and theatre music for the music publishers in Denmark St. During the 1960s pop groups wanting freedom from their record companies' control began to use Regent Sounds as a private venue where they could record in more independent musical styles. The studio gradually became a recognised part of the London music scene.

By the early 1970s Regent Sounds Studio's recording technology had become too basic for modern bands and the business closed. Thereafter the building hosted various businesses including the Helter-Skelter music bookshop before

Music history at Regent Sounds Studios

It is almost quicker to list the music stars of the 1960s who did not record at Regent Sounds Studio. Some were already famous but many were still little known. Eric Clapton and Jeff Beck recorded For Your Love here in 1965 as members of The Yardbirds. The Who recorded the B side of their album A Quick One here. The Kinks recorded many of their early demo albums in the studio. In the very early days of heavy metal music Ozzy Osborne recorded two albums with Black Sabbath here; and an album of Stevie Wonder's was mixed in the studio. Other musical history that was made here is still being researched, but it is certain that many of today's musical icons passed through the studio's doors on their way to fame.

A story exists of how in the 1960s the young Mick Jagger made an agreement with then studio manager Bill Farley: if the Rolling Stones were given free studio time to record a demo album, and if the band became famous as a result, they would record their future albums at Regent Sounds Studio. Hands were shaken, the Stones got free use of the studio, and fame and fortune resulted, but nearly 50 years later - so the story goes - they have not yet returned to keep their promise!

Another studio legend concerns American guitarist Jimi Hendrix, who while recording the song Hey Joe here was sent out of the building by the studio engineers because his guitar was "too loud". Apparently it came as a shock to the British to hear Hendrix's wild guitar-playing style, with intentional distortion, feedback and other original sound effects.

Regent Sounds Studio, now a guitar shop

Inside Regent Sounds Studio, with old music newspapers on the walls

becoming a guitar shop in 2004. Aware of the building's musical history, the present owners have renamed the shop Regent Sounds Studio and have decorated the walls with reproductions of articles and covers from the 1960s music magazines The *Beatles Book* and *Beat Instrumental*, which include photographs of a very young Mick Jagger at the microphone. The shop welcomes visits from serious musicians who are interested in the shop's past and its present.

In the basement of no. 4 is the Alley Cat Club, which holds events playing various genres of music including cabaret, ska, rhythm and blues, calypso and rock'n'roll.

Walk west to no. 6, now a guitar shop. This building is another former recording studio, and in the 1970s the Sex Pistols lived in a rat-infested flat on the first floor. Members of other punk bands, such as Siouxsie and the Banshees and The Clash, also stayed there occasionally. The

6 Denmark St, former home of the Sex Pistols

building had an outside toilet which was so filthy that guests were not keen to use it, but Sid Vicious, Johnny Rotten and the other Pistols were apparently not discouraged. Perhaps the building's hygiene standards improved after the members of the female group Bananarama moved in in 1981. The Pistols' toilet remains at the back of the shop, its walls still covered with the band's graffiti. Sadly it is not available for visual, photographic or physical use by the public, however urgent your need.

In the band's former flat on the first floor, the rats are gone but still remaining are eight cartoons which Johnny Rotten drew on the walls in anger over a redecoration that was not to his taste. Although some of the flat's walls can be seen from the street, the cartoons are not visible from outside. They include a drawing of the artist himself, complete with a rotten tooth, plus illustrations showing other members of the Sex Pistols and their manager Malcolm McLaren. In November 2011 an article in the respected archaeological magazine *Antiquity* surprised its readers by claiming that the cartoons were a more important archaeological find than Tutankhamen's tomb because they are "a direct and powerful representation of a radical and dramatic movement of rebellion." The worldwide archaeological and artistic communities will be grateful to learn that the flat's current occupiers have no plans to remove the cartoons.

To watch a BBC television report about the cartoons, Google "Johnny Rotten graffiti is important say academics".

Also at no. 6 was graphic design company Hipgnosis which produced covers for adult books until asked by Pink Floyd to design the cover of their album *A Saucerful of Secrets*. They eventually became one of the UK's leading album designers and worked for Led Zeppelin, AC/DC, The Scorpions, ELO and hundreds of others.

Walk west to no. 9 Denmark St, formerly the Giaconda Café and regularly visited by the Sex Pistols and The Clash, among others. There are stories of struggling musicians there eating bread rolls with ketchup because they were unable to afford a filling.

The Giaconda was a good place to be seen. Occasionally music producers used to walk in and recruit musicians there and then to help record albums in the nearby studios; and one report says that David Bowie met his first band here. The premises now house a classy French restaurant, the Giaconda Dining Room.

Walk west to Rose Morris at no. 11, which dates back to 1919 when it was founded by Charles and Leslie Rose and Victor Morris. The shop sells musical instruments and printed music on six floors

Cross to the north side of the road and walk east. No. 20 Denmark St, now Wunjo Guitars, was once Mills Music, where in 1965 Elton John, then known by his un-starlike real name Reginald Dwight, began working as the office tea boy. Four years later, as a professional musician, he and lyricist Bernie Taupin wrote one of their biggest hits, Your Song, here. According to later interviews Taupin wrote the lyrics while having breakfast on the roof of Mills Music. We know it was a sunny day because the song says so; and we even know – we think – what Taupin was eating for breakfast because his original handwritten lyric sheet still exists and is stained with coffee and eggs. Later the same day Elton John spent just 10 minutes setting the lyrics to music. It was 10 minutes well spent, because the song has been judged the 136th best song of all time by Rolling Stone magazine, and has been played millions of times since, notably at Prince William and Kate Middleton's wedding reception party. Look up to the roof of no. 20 and you can see the very place (allegedly, we emphasise) where Bernie Taupin took the roof and kicked off the moss, as his lyrics say.

Walk east to Rhodes at no. 22, one of the oldest guitar shops in Britain, having opened in the late 1960s. In case you wonder how the street can support so many guitar shops, the answer is that they all specialise in different niches (for example, no. 4 specialises in Fender guitars), and they are careful not to invade each other's areas of expertise. This type

Wunjo Guitars, formerly Mills Music where the young Elton John worked

of collaboration is one reason why the street survives with so many independent shops. Another reason is perhaps that the musicians who visit Denmark St are the kind of people who prefer to buy from individual shops rather than big chain stores.

On the first floor of no. 22 since the 1950s is Tin Pan Alley Studio, which boasts a long list of famous clients including the Rolling Stones, The Beatles, Elton John, Simon and Garfunkel, The Who, Jimi Hendrix, George Michael, Paul McCartney, The Bee Gees, Stevie Wonder and Natalie Imbruglia.

Walk to the eastern end of Denmark St, where you will see an open area where David Bowie used to live in a campervan while still too poor to rent a room in Denmark St. To the south-east is St Giles' Church in the Fields, which stands where there was once a village on the road to Oxford.

Turn left into High Holborn. On the left are several Korean shops – the start of a Koreatown?

Turn left again into a small alleyway called Denmark Place. This is a dark hidden corner that appears not to have changed since the 1970s, and one where you sense the Sex Pistols might have felt very much at home. On the right is Enterprise Studios, not a recording studio but a rehearsal studio facility where bands can practise.

Opposite Enterprise Studio's door is an alleyway that leads back to Denmark Place. Go into the alleyway and on its right-hand wall you will see a large board where bands advertise for new members. It seems difficult to imagine great stars being found via a recruitment process like that, but who knows? Paul Weller of The Jam and Style Council reportedly found his way into the music business by the improbable method of playing in a Denmark St café and being "discovered" by a music producer.

Return to Denmark Place and walk west past the rubbish and graffiti, then

Recording studio in Denmark Place

"Musicians wanted" notice board off Denmark St

emerge from your 1970s time machine back into present-day Charing Cross Rd.

The walk officially ends here; Tottenham Court Road tube station is a short way north. If you wish, however, you can now **walk just past the tube station to London's cheap electronics district at the southern end of Tottenham Court Rd**, where there are many small shops selling hi-fis, televisions, cameras and computer equipment. The area has been London's electronics district since the end of World War II when a great deal of surplus army radio and electronic equipment was sold there.

A further five minutes' walk north up Tottenham Court Rd is London's furniture district, located near mainline train stations because people from the provinces used to travel to London by train to do their furniture and home décor shopping. Several fashionable shops are there including Heal's, founded as a bedmaker in 1810, and Terence Conran's Habitat, founded in 1964.

Transport London

Start:	Kings Cross tube station
End:	Warren St tube station (Euston Square is also nearby)
Length:	2.75 miles (4.5 miles)
Time taken:	1.5 – 2 hours
Eat and drink:	There are several restaurants opposite Kings Cross and St Pancras stations, and some food stands in the forecourt of the Euston Station building, but best is the many cheap Indian restaurants in Drummond St near the end of the walk
Includes:	Kings Cross train station, the Metropolitan Line (the world's first underground line), Regent Quarter, London Canal Museum, Kings Place, Kings Cross Central development (Victorian railway architecture), German Gymnasium, St Pancras International train station, Woburn Walk (1820s shops), Elizabeth Garrett Anderson Museum, Euston Station, Drummond St (Indian restaurants)
Best time:	Any. London Canal Museum opening times are Tuesday to Sunday, 10 am – 4.30 pm

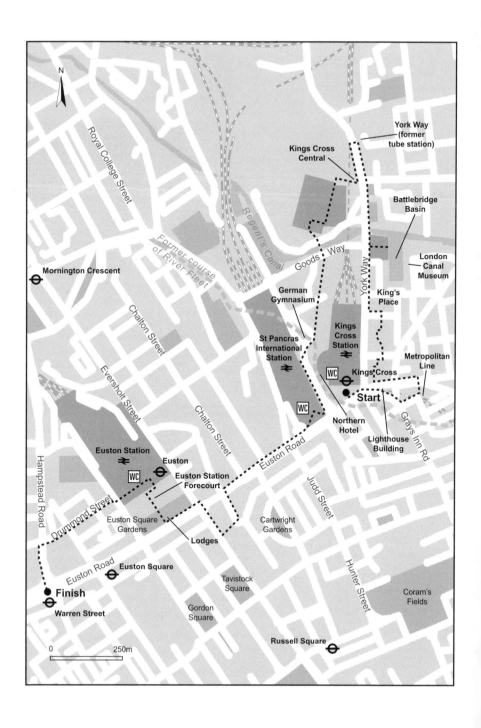

Introduction

It is traditional in Britain to express dissatisfaction with the country's transport system. It was designed for an earlier time, long before the population of these crowded islands reached 62 million, and it often shows its age in the form of breakdowns and delays. London has special difficulty because its population is rising fast, meaning that pressure on the transport network increases constantly.

Every new transport development that is proposed in London meets with support from some but strong opposition from others, and the "planning process", during which new transport suggestions are discussed and everyone is allowed to have their say, takes years and costs a fortune. In the meantime, travellers suffer overcrowded, unreliable and highly-priced transport.

But London has always eventually solved its transport problems, and historically has been responsible for many new transport ideas. On this walk you will see the very first underground train line anywhere in the world, one of London attractive canals, one of the world's most beautiful train stations and one of the dullest, and some of the city's Victorian railway architecture. As you walk, you may happily remember that you are unlikely to suffer delays, overcrowding or expense when you move via the oldest form of transport of all: your feet!

Walk

Kings Cross Train Station

From Kings Cross tube station, exit into the Western Concourse, the station's modernistic ticket hall. In its northern corner is a new pub from where there are good views of the trains,.

Obviously the Western Concourse is modern, but most of the other architecture of Kings Cross is Victorian. If possible, walk into the "shed" (the part of the building where the trains stand). There are in fact two main sheds, side by side. Kings Cross is neither the most beautiful station on this walk nor the worst – those are still to come.

Interior of Kings Cross Station

Exit the station on its southern side. On the outside wall of the building's south-eastern corner there is currently a re-creation of platform 9¾, famous from the Harry Potter books, with a luggage trolley disappearing into the wall, but it may have gone or been moved when you read this.

Platform nine-and-three-quarters, from the Harry Potter books

Stand south of the station's main entrance, near the barriers by Euston Road, and look up to the building's yellow-brick frontage.

In Front of Kings Cross Station

At present the Victorian frontage of the station is being renovated and is mostly

Kings Cross Station, currently being restored

hidden, but hopefully by the time you read this it will be visible again. In front of the Victorian part of the building is an ugly one-storey extension; it was built in 1972 and only intended to be temporary. There are now finally plans to remove it, so it may not be there when you read this.

Look about 50 metres south-east of the station entrance to a busy junction where five roads join. In the "island" in the centre of the junction is the "Lighthouse

The Lighthouse Building under repair, like so much else in this area

building" (also currently being renovated), sometimes alternatively called the "Flatiron building" after the similarly-shaped building in New York, or the "Oysterhouse Building". The lighthouse on its roof was built, according to one theory, as a suitably nautical advertisement for an oyster restaurant below. The whole building is semi-derelict at present, and is an atmospheric reminder of the bad reputation the whole Kings Cross area had in the 1980s – it was virtually a red-light district and had a serious drugs problem. Like much else on this walk the area is in the middle of regeneration at present, so some of what you see on your walk may not be exactly as described here.

The River Fleet used to flow above ground where you are standing (it was converted to run underground through a pipe in Victorian times because of cholera fears). When this area was still countryside the river was crossed by a small bridge known as the "Battlebridge", and when a village developed by the bridge it too took the name Battlebridge. Somehow a legend was formed that the name referred to a battle 2,000 years ago between the invading Romans and the local Iceni tribe led by the Celtic warrior princess Boudicca. The legend is almost certainly untrue, but that did not prevent a mysterious urban myth from arising in recent years that Boudicca's body now lies buried beneath platform 9 of Kings Cross Station.

The whole area was known as Battlebridge until 1836 when a statue of King George IV was erected where the Lighthouse Building now stands, after which it became known as Kings Cross. The statue was removed in 1845 but the name remained.

Although the whole landscape is of course much changed since the Fleet flowed above ground, the river's original bends are still visible in several physical features: the bends of St Pancras Way, the curve in the Northern Hotel, and the curve in Grays Inn Road (see the map of this walk, which shows the river's former course).

Leave the square by its south-eastern corner, past the Hurricane Room (a

former cinema and now a snooker club and casino), and turn left into St Chad's Place. A short way ahead behind a wire fence is a section of the Metropolitan Line. The best place to see it is from the small yard in front of the building marked 44 Wicklow St.

Metropolitan Line

The track below you looks ordinary enough but its importance lies in the fact that it is the oldest underground train line anywhere in the world, dating back to 1863. Not all of it is "underground" – the section you are looking is where the line comes out of a tunnel and runs in the open air, though always below ground level. The early tube engines used steam power, and open-air sections of track were needed so that steam and smoke could escape from the tunnels.

A section of the Metropolitan Line, the world's oldest underground railway

Walk east along St Chad's Place, follow the alley where it bends to the left and emerge into Kings Cross Rd opposite a futuristic-looking house, then turn left and cross to the Poor School, an affordable drama academy created in

Construction of the First Underground Railway

Building an underground railway in the nineteenth century required the invention of new techniques and technology. Tunnel-digging machines did not exist in those days so the "cut and cover" method was planned for the Metropolitan Line's construction: the builders would dig a trench (a long hole), lay the railway track in it, and then cover the line with a strong roof so that roads and houses could be built on top. The problem was that before digging could begin, the land had first to be cleared. Around 1,000 homes in this area were knocked down and as many as 12,000 unlucky occupants forced to move elsewhere, most without compensation (financial help). There were angry claims that the company had intentionally chosen to run the line through poorer areas where local people could not afford to fight for their rights in court.

Once the site was clear, thousands of hard-living "navvies" (diggers) from all over England, Scotland and Ireland arrived and began the long process of digging the trench. As work progressed, countless problems arose: sewers (toilet pipes) and water pipes had to be diverted; a train from Kings Cross fell into the trench causing huge damage; a trench wall collapsed destroying pavements, gardens, telegraph wires and gas and water pipes; and most seriously of all, the River Fleet burst out of its pipes and flooded the line, delaying the project by months.

Despite the difficulties, however, after three years the project was completed, and was an instant success, making further underground rail developments possible in London and elsewhere. There are now around 160 underground railway systems in the world, all of which owe their existence to the original tube line that pioneered the idea and the technology. In fact the word "Metro", used for the underground railways in Paris, Moscow, Tokyo and many other cities, comes from the name of the Metropolitan Line.

The use of the "cut and cover" method explains why the Metropolitan Line is only a little way under the surface of London's streets and can be reached by steps, whereas for other lines that were created by tunnelling machines you need to go much further underground via lift or escalator.

1986. **Go west across Caledonian Rd, then walk north a few metres and stop by a small alleyway on your left with a sign for Varnishers Yard.** This area has recently been named Regent Quarter.

Regent Quarter

Regent Quarter is a small but attractive area of London occupying two blocks, and consisting mostly of Victorian industrial buildings now renovated and converted into cafés, restaurants, offices and flats. Until recently it was closed off and derelict, but with help from the £2 billion regeneration plan for the Kings Cross area it has smartened up considerably.

Go west along the alleyway into Varnishers Yard, now occupied by two Spanish restaurants with colourfully-painted barrels outside. The building on the yard's south side was a factory that made varnish (the colourless liquid painted onto wooden furniture).

Painted barrels in Varnishers Yard

Uses for Nineteenth-Century Railways

Almost all the buildings and yards in Regent Quarter have an obvious industrial past. They were located here because of the nearby railways – they could receive materials from other places in Britain easily, and also could distribute their own products conveniently. One product brought to Kings Cross from other parts of England was coal, some of which must have been used in the industrial yards of what is now Regent Quarter.

If you are English, you have probably heard of Chivers jam. Stephen Chivers was a nineteenth-century fruit-grower in Cambridge who saw the opportunity which the new railways offered. He set up a jam factory and transported his produce into this area of London by rail, thus creating a brand name which survives to this day. Colman's mustard, Hartley's jam and Lea & Perrins sauce are other famous food names which used this area's nineteenth-century railways so well that their brand names are still famous today.

When much of London's cow population died of disease in the mid-nineteenth century, dairies (milk production centres) all over southern England were able to export milk into London using the railways. It is said that the dairy farmers milked their cows at times which fitted the train timetables.

Leave via the west side of the yard, then go north along Bravington Walk past a gym on your left into another small yard with, on its east side, something still surprisingly uncommon in London: a buffet restaurant.

In the north-eastern corner of the yard is an alleyway; enter it and you will see on the left a small green box whose use you may be able to guess. There are more rats than people in London, and it is said that while in the city you are never more than 10 metres from one. They are thought to live in London's Victorian sewers (toilet pipes), and are difficult to get rid of

because they quickly adapt to, or learn to avoid, the many kinds of poisons that have been tried on them. London's sewers are an absolute Serengeti of wildlife – frogs, eels, worms and funguses of every type feel perfectly at home there.

Walk north out of the alley into Caledonia St. On your left is a building with a "KCL" logo on its fence and sign, referring not to the world-famous academic institution of Kings College London but to the rather less celebrated Kings Cross Laundry, the former occupants here.

Former building of the Kings Cross Laundry

Unconnected with transport but a good place to eat – and a charming and old-fashioned shop just to visit – is KC Continental Stores, which offers huge and cheap hand-made sandwiches, plus a

variety of Italian, Spanish and Portuguese food. **Go to the eastern end of Caledonia St and you will see it on the opposite side of the road.** Afterwards, return to Caledonia St's north side, walk west a few metres and then go north under a modern metal arch into the next part of Regent Quarter. A lane called Albion Walk leads you to a small square with some Victorian machinery on the right. The building on the left was a brassworks.

Continue north through Albion Yard and then enter yet another square. The building on the right was a copperworks, and the long building on the left was an ironworks, built in 1866. The top part of its chimney appears to have been rebuilt, as its brickwork looks much newer. In fact the whole Regent Quarter site has been developed with great sensitivity to its past, with help from English Heritage.

Exit the square on its north side into Railway St. Walk west to York Way, then turn right and walk north to Wharfdale Rd. If you want to visit the London Canal Museum (see description below), walk east

Old-fashioned continental food shop near Kings Cross

Former ironworks in Albion Yard

along Wharfdale Rd then north up New Wharf Rd to the museum. Afterwards you will need to return to York Way.

[P07-005small]
Otherwise, cross to the west side of York Way. Stand at the top of a ramp leading down to the back of Kings Cross Station where you have a good view of the train sheds to the south, and, to the north...

Kings Place, art and performance centre

Kings Cross Station train sheds

... the tunnels which take trains under Regent's Canal.

Train lines disappearing into a tunnel under Regent's Canal

Cross back to the east side of York Way and continue north to Kings Place on your right.

Kings Place

Kings Place is known as an arts venue, and is home to two orchestras. It contains two concert halls, a recording studio, rehearsal spaces and several free exhibition halls. The complex is usually open and you are welcome to go in and look around. In the main lobby is a café and the excellent Rotunda restaurant. Artwork is on display on the ground floor and on floors -1 and -2, reachable via escalator, lift or stairs.

Walk to the east side of the main lobby and go through the doors to Battlebridge Basin, part of Regent's Canal.

Regent's Canal

Regent's Canal opened in 1802, when this area was not central London as it is now but outside the city. The canal's aim was to connect the Midlands, Britain's industrial heartland, with the Thames and hence the world. This was before the railway age, and roads were generally extremely poor quality, so water-based transport, whether by canal or sea, was often the only option.

Battlebridge Basin on the Regent's Canal

In the beginning the canal was successful but it was hit hard by the introduction of the railways and by improvements to roads. There was even talk of removing the water from the canal and laying a railway line in its place, though nothing came of this – as you can see.

Canal use increased during the Second World War but thereafter fell back, and by the 1960s commercial traffic had ended almost completely. Nowadays the canal is used mainly for walking, cycling and cruising, though there is a small amount of commercial traffic and attempts are being made to encourage more.

The open water in front of you is Battlebridge Basin, built for the loading and unloading of goods – most of the buildings around its edge were warehouses for the storage of cargo to be transported by canal. Often an entire family would live on the barge and help with the heavy work of loading it. Children received only the most basic education at the Boatman's Institute in west London. Because of their nomadic life and small amount of contact with outsiders, canal people were described as "almost as much a separate class as the gypsies" (quote transliterated into easier English).

You will probably see several beautifully restored barges floating in the basin in front of you. Despite – or perhaps because of – the slow speed of canal life, there is great demand in London for a barge and a place to moor it. In some locations you can only visit your barge during the day, and not live in it permanently.

You may be able to smell coal smoke coming from the barges, a rare odour

these days, because, with a very few exceptions, coal fires have been banned in London since 1956 because of the pollution they caused. When coal smoke from millions of London fires mixed with fog from the river, the resulting "pea-soupers" made it impossible to see more than a few metres on the streets. Apparently the reason why policemen wore white gloves when directing traffic was to make them easier to see in fog.

On the east side of the basin is the London Canal Museum, a former ice storage warehouse owned by Carlo Gatti, the nineteenth-century ice-cream tycoon. The museum is well worth a visit but is not reachable from this side.

Regent's Canal entering the Islington Tunnel

Staying by the waterside, walk north past the Rotunda on your left, then west along the canal to the bridge. From there, look east and you can see the canal entering the Islington Tunnel. Canal barges were pulled by horses on the canal paths, but because there was no canal path through the Islington tunnel a dangerous system known as "legging" was used, meaning that the boat-owner lay on his back on top of the barge and "walked" upside-down along the roof of the tunnel to move the barge forward.

Walk up the ramp back to York Way, and continue north over the bridge. Pass on your right Copenhagen St, named after Copenhagen House, nearby residence of the Danish ambassador in the seventeenth century. Continue past the former York Road School, an attractive

London Canal Museum, in a Victorian ice warehouse

yellow-brick Victorian building now converted into flats. **Go north to York Road tube station, a purple-tiled building on your right.**

Italian Ice-Cream in Britain

Carlo Gatti was born in the Italian-speaking part of Switzerland but in around 1847 he moved to London, where he began selling chestnuts and waffles from a small market stall. He did well, and within a few years had his own café-restaurant, the first in Britain to make and sell ice-cream to the public.

Gatti began to import ice from Norway and stored it in his ice warehouse, in a specially-built "ice well" which still exists. From there it was delivered all around London in Gatti's horse-drawn ice carts. He continued to produce large quantities of ice-cream, and brought hundreds of people from his home region of Ticino to British cities to help him sell it. They could often be heard on the streets of Victorian London shouting "Ecco un poco" ("try a little"), an expression that led to their nickname of "hokey pokey men", which may in turn have inspired the children's song The Hokey Cokey (though there are many other theories as to its origin). The ice-cream sold in London was not always very fresh, and a buyer could never be sure exactly what it was made from, but it was popular nonetheless.

To hear and see The Hokey Cokey, search on YouTube for "hokey cokey tfortimtim".

Italians in London thus became linked with ice-cream, an association that still continues, as demonstrated by the number of Italian ice-cream companies still in existence in Britain, including Greco Brothers Ltd, founded by three brothers from Arpino in Italy; Minghella Ice Cream (film director Anthony Minghella is the son of the business's founders); Rea's Ices (founded by the father of singer Chris Rea); plus Rossi, Marcantonio, Criminisi and others.

York Road Tube Station

If you are tired and were hoping to cut your walk short by catching a train home from this station, prepare yourself for a disappointment. The last train left in 1932. York Road is one of London's 43 "ghost stations", tube stations that have now closed. York Road opened in 1906 but because it was in a lightly-populated industrial area was never much used. However, recently there have been many calls from politicians for its reopening because of the increase in population that will result from all the new housing developments nearby.

York Road station – unused for now

It is only the station that has closed – the Piccadilly Line still runs far below, and from the train you can still see remains of the station below ground if you look carefully. The platform space is clearly visible, as is some of the tiling and a small signalling cabin.

By the York Road station building is Transeuropean Carriage, a car hire company that specialises in left-hand drive vehicles, no doubt targeting its services at travellers arriving from mainland Europe by rail into St Pancras International.

Walk a little further north to the street sign that reads Randell's Rd. From here you have a good view to the north-east of a train line disappearing into – or if you prefer, coming out of – a long grey pipe-like tunnel; this carries Eurostar trains to Paris, Brussels and beyond. Turning to the south you have a view of the tower of St Pancras station and of the London Eye, the Ferris wheel by the Thames, which is four miles south.

Eurostar train heading for Paris

The Kings Cross Central Development site, currently. Image © Simon Hazelgrove

Cross to the west side of York Way and walk south, then stop at the corner of Handyside Rd on your right, where you will see Kings Cross Central.

Kings Cross Central

At the time of writing, Kings Cross Central is still under construction but perhaps by the time you read this most or all of it will be complete. It is an enormous development on the site of old railway lands that have been derelict for decades. Plans include the building of 2,000 homes, 23 office buildings, shops, restaurants, an art college, ten parks, 20 new streets, theatres, cinemas – virtually a whole new town.

Several historic buildings exist on the site and will be preserved in the development. On the southern side of Handyside Rd is a series of nineteenth-century railway structures, now mostly derelict but soon to be renovated as part of the development programme.

Walk west to the first structure (the easternmost), which curves north-westwards. This is the East Handyside Canopy, originally built to cover a road and train track. Joined onto its west side, set back a little way south of the road, is the Midland Goods Shed, which was Kings Cross's main passenger station for two years before the present Kings Cross Station was built. It is to become a shopping centre. Connected onto its west

Projection post-development. Image © Miller Hare

side is the West Handyside Canopy, which has a silver-coloured metal roof. **An old train line leading south is visible on the ground. Follow it south if you are allowed to; otherwise, you will need to return to return to York Way and go south then west along Goodsway.**

If you are able to follow the old train line, continue south almost to the end of the West Handyside Canopy, then go through the doors on the right that lead into an enormous atrium (hall), formerly a goods exchange depot, now part of the University of the Arts London. **Leave the atrium via the doors on its southern**

side, and walk south into the university's reception area.

In the south-west corner of the reception area is a visitors centre with helpful leaflets about Kings Cross Central. In front of it on a table is an interactive model of the development with buttons you can press to learn about it.

Walk south out of the building, past the old train line on your right, and continue over the canal bridge to Goodsway. If possible, walk south down Kings Boulevard towards St Pancras. Otherwise, walk west along Goodsway then turn south down Pancras Rd.

At the time of writing, there are no buildings on Kings Boulevard, but a great many shops, offices and hotels are planned; there may even be trams (street trains).

How Kingsway is expected to look one day. Image © Miller Hare

As you reach the southern end of Kings Boulevard, on the left you will see the outside of the Western Concourse of Kings Cross.

On your right is the German Gymnasium, a former gym which now houses Kings Cross Central's marketing suite.

On display inside the Gymnasium is a large scale model of the proposed developments on the site, and there is an exhibition of the plans at the rear of the building. If the building is closed you can see the model through the front window.

Continue south to St Pancras International. Walk west up the steps in the south-eastern corner of the station complex, and stand where you can see the front of the building properly.

The German Gymnasium, home of Kings Cross Central's marketing office

St Pancras International

St Pancras is one of the most magnificent train stations you are ever likely to see. Its sophisticated Victorian Gothic design was intended to show its superiority over Kings Cross, which was owned by a competitor rail company. The part of the building you are now looking at was the Midland Grand Hotel, now renamed the St Pancras Renaissance London Hotel, with the station behind it.

Incredibly, this spectacular building was nearly demolished in the 1960s. Most of its train services had moved to other stations, and St Pancras was so little used that many Londoners did not even know the building was a train station. It only escaped destruction after a determined fight led by poet John Betjeman. For many years the station remained in a kind of limbo, only finding a new role in 2007 as the terminus for rail services to mainland Europe. This involved a long and costly

Grand frontage to St Pancras International

Unmissable statue in St Pancras station

renovation, but everyone agrees the result is marvellous.

Enter the main part of the station. In the south-eastern corner is a pub called the Betjeman Arms, named after the station's saviour.

Nearby under the station clock is a large statue of a man embracing a woman with an interesting design around the bottom.

Apologies, let us try that once more. We meant to say that on the large statue of the man and woman embracing you will see an interesting frieze (long design) around the bottom – the bottom of the statue. The creator, British sculptor Paul Day, said he wanted the drama of the frieze to contrast with the idealised vision of the couple above.

Look up to the enormous arched shed roof, the largest in the world when it was built, using a round wooden frame as a base.

Below it on the main floor level are the Eurostar trains which speed back and forth between London and cities on the European mainland.

Looking down below floor level you can see the former undercroft (basement), now a shopping arcade but previously a storage area for beer transported from Staffordshire (the pillars you see were intentionally spaced to allow exactly three barrels of beer between them).

You may wonder why the trains at Kings Cross leave from street level while those

St Pancras undercroft, formerly for beer storage, now a shopping centre

of St Pancras leave from one level higher. The reason is that the trains from Kings Cross go under Regents Canal, while those from St Pancras go over it via a bridge.

On the western side of the station is a statue of Sir John Betjeman, apparently looking in admiration at the huge train shed. Engraved into the floor are some lines from his poem Cornish Cliffs. A little way north is the longest champagne bar in Europe.

Sir John Betjeman, whose campaigning saved the station from demolition

Walk to the south-western corner of the station to a bar called Booking Office. Needless to say, this was the station's actual booking office where tickets were sold, and it contains many original features including beautiful wood panelling on the walls. By the bar's north-western exit is a doorway leading to a hotel corridor. A short way north along that corridor is a lift which you may be able to take to the seventh floor, from where there are good views of the building's rooftops.

Go into the room just west of the Booking Office; this is now the hotel reception but was formerly a place where horse-drawn carriages dropped off their passengers. Exit via the southern door into the station's driveway. As you walk down the hill you can see on your right the hotel's Gilbert Scott Restaurant, named after the building's nineteenth-century architect, who deserves to be better remembered today, especially as he designed or altered over 800 other buildings.

At the bottom of the driveway, stand by Euston Rd.

Euston Rd

Euston Rd was built in the 1740s as London's first bypass, that is, a road designed to take traffic around a busy area instead of through it. In those days the "traffic" was mostly sheep and cattle on their way to market, which the eighteenth-century rich hated as an uncivilised rustic invasion and wanted kept away from their streets. Today Londoners would probably greet such a sight with absolute delight. In fact as recently as the 1920s farmers walked flocks of sheep through the streets of central London, normally to a train station for transportation. At around the same time, the grass in London's parks was kept short by a flock of sheep brought specially from Scotland.

In 1846 the government passed a law preventing train lines from going south of Euston Road, which is why there are five major terminals on its north side: Kings Cross, St Pancras, Euston, Marylebone and Paddington.

From St Pancras station walk west, passing the British Library on your right, where there are often free exhibitions you can visit. A little further west at Chalton St there is a lively street market on Fridays, which is very helpful information for you if today is Friday. Chalton St is a working-class area that is rapidly gentrifying (becoming more fashionable), no doubt helped by the Kings Cross regeneration.

On the corner of Euston Rd and Chalton Street is a pub called The Rocket, named

The Rocket pub, Chalton Street

after one of the earliest steam trains in the world, built in 1829 and now on display in the London Science Museum.

Continue west from Chalton St to the former Elizabeth Garrett Anderson Hospital, named after the first woman in Britain to gain a medical qualification. From Wednesday to Friday you can visit the building's free exhibition about her life and the struggles of women to enter the medical profession.

Cross to the south side of Euston Rd and walk south into Dukes Rd, with its attractive 1820s buildings on the right. At the southern end of the road look southeast and you will see an unusual shop, the Maghreb Bookshop with its name in English and French.

Nineteenth-century shop buildings in Dukes Road

Go west along Woburn Walk, where there are more well-preserved nineteenth-century shop buildings, now occupied by restaurants, bookshops and galleries.

At the end of Woburn Walk, turn right and go north past St Pancras Parish Church, where free lunchtime concerts are regularly held. **Cross to the north side of Euston Rd where you see the 1902 fire station, then cross to the north-west corner of the junction, then continue west and stop by the westernmost of the two white lodge gates of Euston Station.**

Shop fronts in Woburn Walk

Euston Station

The two lodges beside you are occupied by the pub the Euston Tap; the western lodge specialises in beers from around the world, and the eastern one specialises in cider. That may be useful, because what you need now is a stiff drink. You are about to see what happens when a beautiful Victorian train station is destroyed and a modern version built in its place. These lodge buildings and the war memorial just north of them are

Lodge buildings from the former Euston Station

almost all that remains of the old station on this site.

Engraved on the walls of the lodges are the names of towns with rail connections to Euston. From the westernmost lodge walk north, with the bus station on your right. Continue north till you reach the station forecourt, which is full of convenience food stalls and restaurants, and stand by the only other survivor from the original station, a statue of Robert Stephenson, who with his father built the Rocket stream train that we just referred to.

Destinations reachable from Euston

Something which used to stand near here but was destroyed along with the original station is the much-missed Euston Arch, a piece of monumental railway architecture that resembled the Arc de Triomphe in Paris and served as the entrance to the original station. There is now a movement to rebuild the arch using the original stones, whose various locations have now mostly been discovered after years of searching. The arch's ornamental metal

gates were taken to the York Railway Museum. Some of the stones are now in the gardens of those involved with the destruction, but most were used to fill a river channel in East London. Recently, the river was dredged (made deeper) as part of the development work for the 2012 London Olympic Games, and some of the stones have been recovered from the water in good condition, giving hope to the idea that the arch will one day rise again, just as Temple Bar did (see the Legal London walk).

To see a 10-minute video of how historian Dan Cruickshank found some of the arch's stones in a builder's garden, search on YouTube for "The Euston Arch: Dan Cruickshank searching for the remains".

To see an 8-minute video of how, to his great delight, he found one of the arch's stones in the River Lea, search on YouTube for "Euston Arch: Dan Cruickshank finds piece in the River Lea" (the joke in that video's title seems intentional).

It is worth entering Euston Station to see the contrast between it and London's surviving Victorian stations. Go inside the main building. The station concourse (shopping and ticket area) is separate from the train level, which is reached via ramps on the north side. Walk down one of the ramps and you will see that the train area was designed without daylight and with a very low ceiling; this was because space was needed for the huge postal depot above.

The new station concourse in Euston Station

From Euston Station every night runs one of Britain's last two night train services, the Caledonian Sleeper, which connects London with several Scottish cities. If you would like to spend the weekend in Scotland you can leave your office in rainy London on a Friday evening, get on the night train at Euston, and open your curtains the next morning to see a different world rushing past outside your window: fresh air, open spaces, red deer running across the rolling Scottish hills... though there is no guarantee you will have escaped the rain.

The Great Architecture Debate

Whereas St Pancras station was saved from destruction, the original at Euston was not so lucky. The present characterless building is a 1960s replacement of the original 1837 structure, which was found to be "inadequate" (not enough), though it seems more probable that the station was a victim of the general desire for "modernisation" in the 1960s, which saw the destruction of countless Victorian buildings and medieval town centres all over Britain, their place mostly taken by concrete structures that now look dirty and worn. It is worth noting that the towns and cities in Britain that attract the most tourists, and where house prices are highest, are the ones whose centres largely escaped "modernisation", such as York, Bath, Durham, Oxford, Cambridge and others. The architectural tastes of the 60s are generally regretted today.

There is of course an alternative argument, which is that architecture has to change and move on, just as society does. Would it really make sense to build in the Victorian style today? Should all periods of a city's history not leave their mark in architecture, rather than trying to lock an entire city in one particular period forever? Is London not a more interesting city for its mix of architectural styles than, say, Paris, whose centre is uniformly mid-nineteenth century? Will Euston Station one day seem as beautiful as St Pancras?

Leave Euston Station via its north-western entrance, between the Boots and Journey's Friend shops, and walk west past the British Transport Police station into a small yard and then out into Melton St.

On the corner of Melton St and Drummond St is a former entrance to Euston tube station, relocated inside the station in the 1960s when escalators began to be used.

Former entrance to Euston tube station, now unused

Stand on the corner of Melton St and Drummond St.

Drummond St

Drummond St used to extend much further east, but it was cut in half when the new Euston Station was built. Other than that it has no transportational relevance, but it is worth a visit for its numerous cheap Indian restaurants, whose tantalising aromas you have by now probably noticed for yourself.

The vegetarian restaurants of Drummond Street

Walk to the western end of Drummond St where you see the Camden People's Theatre, a small community theatre focussing on "adventurous" performances. **Cross to the west side of Hampstead Rd then walk south.** This is one of the windiest corners in London – your author studied near here for three years and never walked this way without feeling as though he was inside a tornado. **Continue south over the busy crossroads to Warren St tube station, where the walk ends.**

Clever London

Start:	Euston Square tube station (Warren St and Euston are also nearby)
End:	Tottenham Court Road tube station
Length:	1.5 miles (2.5 kilometres)
Time taken:	1 hour, but you may want to stop at the several free museums and galleries along the way which are relevant to the walk
Eat and drink:	You will pass many low-cost student canteens. The Print Room Café in the Wilkins Building is recommended
Includes:	Grant Museum of Zoology (Victorian science museum), Wilkins Building, body of Jeremy Bentham, UCL Archaeology Collections, Petrie Museum of Egyptian Archaeology, SOAS Brunei Gallery, former workplace of TS Eliot, house where Oscar Wilde stayed, Senate House (inspiration for George Orwell's Ministry of Truth), British Museum and former Reading Room, Cartoon Museum, Florida State University London Campus

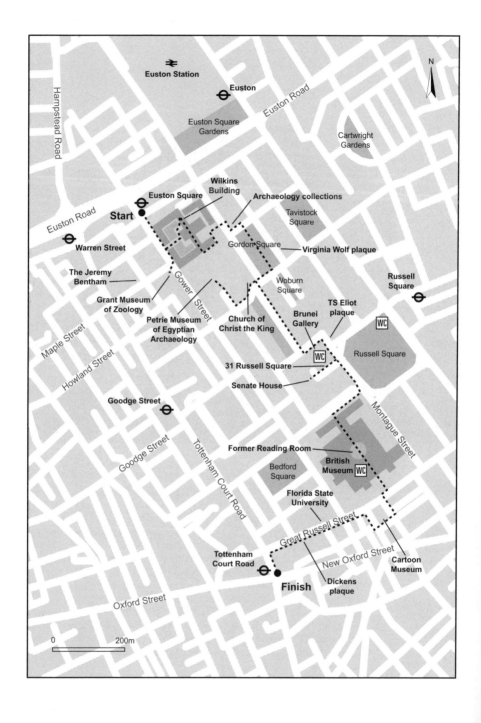

Best time: The student areas of the walk are more lively during term time. The museums on the walk have limited opening times, currently as follows: Grant Museum of Zoology, Monday to Friday 1 - 5 pm; UCL Archaeology Collections, Monday to Friday 9 am - 5 pm); Petrie Museum of Egyptian Archaeology, Tuesday to Saturday 1 - 5 pm; Brunei Gallery, Tuesday to Saturday 10.30 am - 5 pm, open till 8 pm Thursday); British Museum, every day 10 am - 5.30 pm, Thursday until 8.30 pm; Cartoon Museum, Tuesday to Saturday 10.30 am - 5.30 pm, Sunday 12 noon - 5.30 pm. All except the British Museum are closed on public holidays

Introduction

If London has a "clever" district, it is the leafy squares and student campuses of Bloomsbury. Not only is it associated with numerous writers including Dickens, TS Eliot, Dorothy L Sayers, Oscar Wilde and the Bloomsbury Group but it is also home to the British Museum and the University of London.

You may be surprised how much of the University of London is open to the public on weekdays during term-time. On this walk you can recreate your student days by enjoying the intellectual and studious college atmosphere – if that was what you did as a student. You may even be able to visit a lecture (university lesson), depending when you do the walk. You can also enjoy the subsidised food and drink at the student cafés and restaurants, or even a free meal from Hare Krishna.

As you walk around Bloomsbury, taking care to avoid the many student bicycles, you are following in the footsteps of world leaders who studied at the University of London including four monarchs, 52 presidents or prime ministers and 72 Nobel prize winners, plus hundreds of other successful artists, authors, classical musicians, film directors, explorers and businesspeople. If it's clever, it happens here.

Walk

From **Euston Square tube station**, take the southern exit (turn left after you walk through the ticket machines) and walk south down Gower St. After 200 metres you will see on your left the white classical frontage of the **Wilkins Building**, part of University College London (UCL), and on your right the red Victorian brick of the **Cruciform**, a building completed in 1906 as a hospital but since 1995 part of UCL. The building was designed in a cross shape to allow the maximum light and fresh air into all rooms for the benefit of patients.

Walk south a short way to University St on the right. On the corner is the Grant Museum of Zoology, part of UCL.

The Grant Museum of Zoology

There are thousands of museums in Britain, around 400 of which are owned by universities. Most are used internally for teaching or research but about 100 are regularly open to the public. In some cases a university museum is created when the university buys a private collection; in other cases a rich collector simply gives his collection to a university.

The Grant Museum was founded in 1827 by Robert Edmond Grant, Britain's

UCL's Grant Museum of Zoology

first Professor of Zoology, whose opinions on evolution influenced the young Charles Darwin. Even for those not especially interested in zoology the museum is well worth a visit. Inside it looks like something from an adventure film set in Victorian times. The wooden shelves are filled with stuffed animals, skeletons and exotic creatures preserved in ancient glass bottles. It is easy to imagine a mad Victorian explorer like Professor Challenger bringing weird specimens back home from distant jungles and pickling them all here.

The museum is open Monday to Friday from 1 to 5 pm.

Look west from the front of the Grant Museum and around 150 metres away is the pub The Jeremy Bentham, named after the eighteenth-century philosopher who was one of the inspirations behind the creation of UCL. Later in the walk we will be meeting him in person.

UCL

Return to the gates of UCL which you walked past earlier. The two small gatehouses sometimes contain academic

The Jeremy Bentham pub, named after one of the founders of UCL

exhibitions. Go east through the gate into the main quadrangle (open space), where in front of you are the white pillars of the Wilkins Building, built in 1830. On the north side is the Slade School of Fine Art, one of Britain's top art and design colleges. Walk north-east and enter the Wilkins Building via the small door in the north-east corner of the quadrangle. Inside the building, walk east a few metres to the North Cloisters, a long north-south corridor where there is usually an exhibition. Walk south till you reach the Octagon, an eight-sided hall. Up the steps on the east side is the Jeremy Bentham Room where lectures are sometimes held; a university restaurant called The Terrace is also to be found there.

Continue south from the Octagon into the South Cloisters, where again there are usually exhibitions. On the left as you walk is the roof garden and the Japanese monument, commemorating some of the first Japanese students at UCL in the nineteenth century. By a staircase on your left are signs to the Refectory, where there are several low-cost restaurants. You will probably be able to eat in any of the many student restaurants and cafés you see during the walk.

At the end of the South Cloisters is Jeremy Bentham, as promised. His body was preserved after his death and placed inside a wood and glass case, forever to watch over the university he inspired. In fact the head is a wax replica, and the clothes do not exactly contain the great man's body, just his skeleton.

Now that the Grant Museum of Zoology and the remains of Jeremy Bentham are behind us, we can promise the reader there are no more preserved bodies on this walk.

Near Bentham – guarding him, you might say – are the 5000-year-old Koptos lions, found in pieces in Egypt in 1894, and reconstructed in 1980.

Walk west then south into the South Wing, then go down the stairs. In front of you is the imaginatively-named "UCL Shop"; to your left is the Print Room Café, which serves discounted hot meals. Exit the building on its south side into the open area called South Junction and walk east (the road bends left then right) till you reach Gordon St. As we continue the walk you will see many departments of UCL throughout Bloomsbury, including, at the corner of Gordon St and Gordon Square, the UCL Department of Archaeology, which houses the university's Archaeology Collections.

Archaeology Collections

UCL is fortunate enough to have an archaeology collection of some 80,000 objects, a small number of which are on free display to the public. Anyone can walk in and browse the small gallery at their leisure. At the eastern end of the gallery is a lecture room, and if there is a lecture in progress you will probably be able to sit and listen to it.

Gordon Square, one of the many squares of Bloomsbury

UCL's Archaeology Collections

Even walkers who are not archaeology fanatics will still enjoy having a quick look at the museum and a brief sit-in on a lecture, even if only to see an archaeology teacher in action, passing on grand academic wisdom to all the fresh young faces in front of him.

Gordon Square, one of Bloomsbury's many open areas, is to the south. From the Archaeology Department walk east a short way to the entrance to the gardens, formerly a private park for the square's residents but now owned by UCL and, with true academic idealism, open to everyone. Walk south through the middle of the gardens. You may or may not recognise the east side of Gordon Square from the car chase in the film *The Mummy Returns*, when the bus swerves to avoid a car.

Clearly Gordon Square, with its archaeological connections, is the perfect place to make a film about mummies (meaning "preserved human bodies" – and we absolutely promise that is the last mention of them).

To see the section of *The Mummy Returns* that contains the car chase, search on YouTube for "The Mummy Returns (4/11) Movie CLIP - Mummy Battle on a Bus (2001) HD".

If car chases are too exciting for you, on the houses in the south-east of the square you will see two plaques, one marking the home of economist John Maynard Keynes and the other the Bloomsbury Group, of which he was a member.

Authors Virginia Woolf and EM Forster are the two most famous members of the Bloomsbury Group, a set of mostly upper-class writers, intellectuals and philosophers who were active during the early twentieth century. They were also known for their liberal attitudes towards relationships, of which they had many, in a variety of types. Dorothy L Sayers remarked that the Bloomsbury Group were "pairs who had affairs in squares". Another geometrically-minded joker said that they "lived in squares and loved in triangles". For more information about the group, see the sign on the southern side of Gordon Square, which explains that they "seemed" to move from one partner to another.

At the end of Gordon Square Gardens, walk west along Byng Place, past the Church of Christ the King. When you

reach Malet Place turn right and walk north to the Petrie Museum on your left.

Petrie Museum

The Petrie is a university museum of Egyptian archaeology located in a former stable. You may be surprised to learn that it holds the world's fourth biggest collection of Egyptian items after the Cairo Museum, the British Museum and the Egyptian Museum in Germany. It contains part of Egypt's earliest known calendar, the earliest known piece of metal from Egypt, the world's earliest medical text, the only piece of veterinary papyrus, the largest architectural drawing from ancient Egypt, and the oldest dress from Egypt.

The museum's origins lie in 1873 when successful Victorian author Amelia Edwards went on holiday to Egypt and developed an interest in ancient Egyptian culture. Her book *A Thousand Miles Up the Nile* in 1876 became a bestseller, and she began to campaign for the preservation of Egyptian sites to prevent them being destroyed by tourism. She collected many ancient items and brought them from Egypt to Britain, an act which apparently did not fall into the category of "destroying by tourism". When she died she left her entire collection of artefacts to UCL, and the museum was born.

The collection was expanded in 1913 when UCL bought the collection of William Flinders Petrie, the Indiana Jones of his day. He also removed a great many objects from Egypt but only because, he said, he was shocked at the lack of interest in preserving them locally. He described the situation as a "house on fire", and felt he had to save the items before more were lost.

As with UCL's Archaeology Collections, you do not need to be an archaeology fanatic to enjoy the Petrie. Even a short visit is enough to give you the feel of the museum.

Return to Byng Place and walk south down Torrington Square, where a farmers market is held on Thursdays. The skyscraper ahead of you is Senate House. At the end of Torrington Square turn left and on the south-eastern corner of the square you will see the Brunei Gallery, part of SOAS, UCL's School of Oriental and African Studies.

If it is around 1 pm, you will see a long line of students queuing up for their free

UCL's Petrie Museum of Egyptian Archaeology

Farmers Market in Torrington Square

Students queuing for free Hare Krishna food

Hare Krishna meal. You are welcome to join the end of the line.

Brunei Gallery

The gallery was funded by the Sultan of Brunei, one of the world's richest men. Inside is a tiny academic bookshop and three floors of exhibition space housing exhibitions relating to the parts of the world that SOAS studies. On the building's roof is a Japanese garden intended as a place of "quiet contemplation and meditation", which is perhaps why no students are usually found there. The exhibitions and garden are free to visit.

After visiting the Brunei Gallery, walk east to the end of the road and turn right, and immediately on your left you will see a plaque on the wall of 24 Russell Sq, which informs us that poet TS Eliot used to work for publishers Faber and Faber here. Eliot has been called one of the most important poets of the twentieth century, but as with so many other great artists he is best remembered today for his lightest and most playful work: a set of poems he wrote for his grandchildren, *Old Possum's Book of Practical Cats*, set to music by at least three composers including Andrew Lloyd Webber in his musical *Cats*.

The Brunei Gallery, part of UCL's School of Oriental and African Studies

Former workplace of poet TS Eliot

Go south a short way then walk west in the direction of Senate House. On the right at no. 31 Russell Square is the house where author and playwright Oscar Wilde spent his last night in London before leaving Britain for France, where he lived in poverty for three years till his death in 1900.

Senate House – Big Brother is watching you

House where Oscar Wilde stayed on his last night in London

Senate House

Senate House is a 1937 Art Deco skyscraper designed by architect Charles Holden, who also designed some of London's tube stations.

Today the building has sinister associations that were not intended at the time of its construction. Its style has been called "Stalinist", perhaps because of its towering height, its strong shape, its lack of detail and its large number of narrow prison-like windows. However, if the building is "Stalinist", it influenced Stalin rather than vice versa, because it was built before Stalin came to power in the Soviet Union, and before the construction of similar buildings in Eastern Europe such as the "Seven Sisters" in Moscow and the Palace of Culture in Warsaw (pictured on next page).

During World War II Senate House was the government's Ministry of Information, and it inspired the Ministry of Truth in George Orwell's dystopian novel *Nineteen Eighty-four*. Anyone who has read the book and knows of the building's role in it might feel a shiver down their spine as they walk past Senate House. Is Big Brother watching you from those narrow windows on the seventeenth floor? Which cold-eyed bureaucrat sits inside rewriting history to fit the latest party line? Are the Thought Police about to tap you on the shoulder?

Thankfully Orwell's terrible vision of the future has not come true, and Senate House is full of nothing more evil than

Warsaw's Palace of Culture

cheery students from all over the world. You can enter and walk around most of the ground floor, which contains many period Art Deco features.

Go back to Russell Square and walk south, then go west on Montague Place to the rear entrance of the British Museum. A van selling African food is usually parked outside.

African food on sale outside the British Museum

British Museum

Our policy is to discuss a sight only briefly if there is plentiful information available elsewhere, so we will pass quickly through the British Museum, describing only the famous Reading Room.

Enter the north door of the museum in Montague Place and walk south through the exhibition rooms till you reach Great Court, a huge open hall. The round structure in the centre houses the iconic Reading Room, built in 1857 and formerly the main reading room of the British Library. A great many famous people have read there including Karl Marx, Lenin, Gandhi, Rudyard Kipling, Mark Twain, HG Wells, and some friends we have met already on this walk: Oscar Wilde, George Orwell and Virginia Woolf.

Nowadays the Reading Room is open only for exhibitions, but it has been used as a backdrop for several films including the Hitchcock thriller *Blackmail*. To see that part of the film, search on YouTube for "blackmail hitchcock british museum".

Walk south out of the British Museum's main entrance, then go west along Great Russell St, south down Museum St then west on Little Russell St to the Cartoon Museum.

Cartoon Museum

London's Cartoon Museum in Little Russell Street

The Cartoon Museum houses a collection of British cartoons and comic magazines, and displays constantly changing exhibitions. One previous exhibition was "Ronald Searle", named for the artist who drew the original cartoons of St Trinian's School, full of wild and anarchic schoolgirl vandals. The several recent St Trinian's films have been comedies but the original cartoons were rather darker. Some showed the girls carrying weapons such as knives, guns and grenades; others showed the dead bodies of girls who had been killed on the school sports fields. The museum is open every day except Monday.

Walk west to Coptic St then north back to Great Russell St, then continue west. On the right at no. 99 is Florida State University's London campus, which exists so that students from the Sunshine State can experience a year of study in a foreign country – but not a country that is so foreign that time must be wasted learning another language first. FSU's web site promotes the London campus by saying it is near the National Gallery, the British Museum, and opera and ballet theatres, so obviously the web site is aimed not at the students but at their parents, who are presumably paying the fees.

A number of other American colleges have campuses in Bloomsbury including the universities of California, Delaware and New York. You may have heard many American accents while walking around Bloomsbury.

A little further west at no. 14 on the south side of the road is a plaque marking the home of one of Charles Dickens' characters. Many sources say that Dickens lived in the house, but this is incorrect. The only one of Dickens' many London houses that survives is 48 Doughty St (nearby in Bloomsbury but not on this walk), which is now home to the Charles Dickens Museum. Dickens was considered one of Victorian Britain's greatest writers, and is remembered especially for his concern for social reform.

Florida State University's London campus

One writer who did live at 14 Great Russell St was Welsh author WH Davies, best known for his autobiography *Supertramp*, the story of his low-cost wanderings through the United States in the late nineteenth century. He used to commit crimes specifically so that he could spend the winter in prison being fed at the government's expense.

Our minds improved, we end this Clever London walk at Tottenham Court Road tube station, a short walk west then south.

Legal London

Start:	Chancery Lane tube station
End:	St Paul's tube station
Length:	2 miles (3.25 kilometres)
Time taken:	1.5 hours with no stops, but a visit mid-walk to see an English court in session is highly recommended
Eat and drink:	The George pub in the Strand is an atmospheric choice for lunch, as is the 350-year-old Cheshire Cheese in the same street. A few restaurants are located around St Paul's
Includes:	Staple Inn (400-year-old legal premises), Grays Inn (the four "inns" on this walk are attractive districts of lawyers' offices and other historic buildings), Lincoln's Inn, Ede & Ravenscroft (lawyers' clothing and wig shop), Field House Tribunals (court), Royal Courts of Justice, Middle Temple, Inner Temple, Dr Johnson's House (museum, former home of Samuel Johnson, writer of the first English dictionary), Cheshire Cheese (350-year-old pub and restaurant), the "Old Bailey" (Central Criminal Court), St Paul's Cathedral

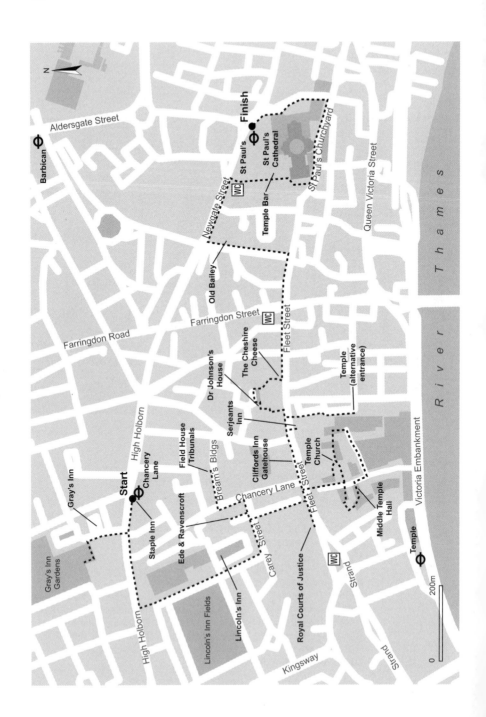

Best time:	Any, but if you want to see a court in session, read the opening times and telephone to confirm: Field House Tribunals: open Monday to Friday 9 am - 5 pm, closed on public holidays, call 0845 600 0087; Royal Courts of Justice, open Monday to Friday from 9 am, courts operate from 10.30 am - 1 pm then 2 - 4.30 pm, closed on public holidays, call 020 7947 6000; Central Criminal Court (the Old Bailey), open Monday to Friday 10 am - 1 pm then 2 - 5 pm, closed public holidays and every bank holiday plus the following day, reduced opening times apply in August, call 020 7248 3277. Note that children under 14 will not be allowed to enter the courtrooms

Introduction

The English legal system dates back hundreds of years, and many aspects of it today seem almost charmingly old-fashioned: the judge's robes (clothing), the lawyers' wigs (artificial hair), the use of Latin legal phrases, and the existence of ancient laws still in force today (the oldest dates from 1267). England's justice system has been exported to many countries, and English courts are still the final decision-making bodies for several Commonwealth countries.

English law may be ancient and dusty, but this walk is not. We will visit some of the places in London's legal district, many of which are beautiful and little known, and are in fact often used as film locations. We will drink in pubs with lawyers and see the shops where judges buy their wigs and gowns. Best of all, we will visit court buildings where you can actually enter a courtroom and watch real criminal trials happening.

Walk

Staple Inn

Leave Chancery Lane tube station via exit 3, and directly in front you will see the black and white frontage of Staple Inn.

An "inn" is an old word meaning a hotel. From around 500 years ago several inns were set up in this part of London where lawyers could live, study and work, and this is still the capital's legal district today. We will visit the four inns that are still in operation, all in handsome historic locations.

Tudor frontage of Staples Inn

If there are relatively few old buildings left in London, it is because they have had to survive so much over the years. Since Staple Inn was built in 1585 it has had to deal with the Great Fire of London in 1666, a fire in the building next door, and, in 1922, an attack of death-watch beetles, insects which can destroy buildings by living in and eating wood. In 1944 the roof was destroyed in a bombing raid, and ten years passed before it was renovated. It is now used as offices.

Cross the road to the north side of High Holborn and walk west, stopping at the archway marked Grays Inn, just before the Cittie of Yorke pub at no. 22.

Grays Inn

Perhaps millions of people have walked past this ordinary-looking archway

Entrance to Gray's Inn

South Square, Grays Inn

without realising that beyond it is a beautiful collection of buildings – almost like a small town – as well as a lovely park.

Grays Inn is one of the surviving four inns; in order to work as a barrister (lawyer) you need to be a member of an inn. Grays was founded on this site probably before 1370 with a manor house (aristocratic home), and further buildings were gradually added. The current buildings date from various different eras; many have been reconstructed since World War II when they suffered serious bomb damage.

Walk north through the main archway and past the security gate into South Square with its statue of Francis Bacon, a polymath (expert in many subjects) who was associated with the inn. The building on the square's north side is Grays Inn Hall, located on the site of the original manor house. It contains an ancient table carved from the wood of warships of the Spanish Armada, which attacked England in 1588. The fact that England owns tables that were carved from the ships' wood tells you the attack was unsuccessful.

Continue north to Grays Inn Square, and from its south-western corner go west along Field Court. On your right is The Walks, a quiet and attractive park area which you can enter on weekdays. Near the end of Field Court on your left is Warwick Court, where on an east wall a plaque marks the former house of Sun Yat-sen, the Chinese revolutionary leader who lived here while in political exile.

The Walks, attractive park area in Grays Inn

If Warwick Court is open, walk south back to High Holborn; otherwise, return the way you came. When you reach High Holborn cross to the south side of the road and walk west to a small alleyway called Great Turnstile. Follow it south to Lincoln's Inn Fields, London's largest public square. On your left is one of the red-brick buildings of Lincoln's Inn. Walk past it to the Gatehouse, which is the main entrance.

Lincoln's Inn

The beautiful Lincoln's Inn is the second of the four inns on this walk. The Gatehouse where you are now standing is the oldest structure on the site, built in 1521. The red-brick building just north of you is New Hall, built in the nineteenth century after it was decided the original Old Hall, built in 1489 and still standing today, was too small for the inn's growing membership.

Quiet area in Lincoln's Inn

New Hall in Lincoln's Inn

The gardens of Lincoln's Inn can be visited from 7 am to 7 pm, and the chapel between 12 noon and 2.30 pm.

In theory the other areas of Lincoln's Inn are not open to the public, but if anyone at the Gatehouse asks, you can say you are going to visit the gardens, and in practice probably no one will mind if you walk quietly around the other parts of the inn.

Main square in Lincoln's Inn

If you are unable to enter Lincoln's Inn, all is not lost – two more inns feature in the walk later.

From the Gatehouse, continue south along Serle St to Carey St, where you will see in front of you the back of the huge Royal Courts of Justice. The expression "on Carey St" used to mean "bankrupt", because the bankruptcy courts were located here.

Seven Stars

Turn left and walk east along Carey St. On your left is the pub Seven Stars, with an eccentric legal-related window display which includes stuffed mice and animal skeletons. The pub was built in 1602 and survived the Great Fire of London. Inside the pub you feel the year could still be 1602, because much of the building seems ancient and the stairs are atmospherically narrow.

On the walls are posters of films that used the building as a background location. At lunchtimes the pub is a good place for the sport of people-watching (and -listening) because it is usually full of dynamic lawyers from the nearby chambers (legal firms) discussing their work.

The pub's cat, often dressed as a lawyer, is a star attraction.

Continue east along Carey St. On your left, just before the legal bookshop Wildy & Sons, is another entrance to Lincoln's

The pre-Fire The Seven Stars pub, with a legal theme

Inn, where you may be able to enter if you had no luck at the Gatehouse.

Then continue east on Carey St and turn left into Star Yard, where on the right you will see one of the entrances to Ede & Ravenscroft.

Ede & Ravenscroft

Ede & Ravenscroft was established in 1689 and is London's oldest tailor. The business makes, hires and sells clothing for barristers, judges, church and parliamentary officials, mayors and university staff and graduates, not just in Britain but in countries worldwide, especially former British colonies. Over the centuries they have provided the robes for twelve British coronations.

Clothing for the legal profession is not a simple matter. The type of wig you wear depends on what type of judge you are, or how senior a lawyer you are. The choice of robe depends on which court you are in, which season of the year it is, whether it is a special occasion, and whether the trial is civil or criminal. As a further complication, many other countries including Scotland, Ireland, Australia, Canada, Hong Kong, Pakistan and India have systems of court uniform adapted from, but not exactly the same as, the English versions.

Wigs in Court

The tradition of wearing wigs in courts dates back hundreds of years. In sixteenth-century English society men often wore long curly wigs because they were considered attractive, but they also had a hygienic use. Head lice (insects) were common, but by shaving his hair and wearing a wig a man could become lice-free. A wig was also a sign of wealth. In the late eighteenth century, shorter wigs became more fashionable, and the style of wig used in English courts dates from that time. By 1820, wigs had gone out of fashion completely, but remained in use in courts.

According to some people, wigs make judges look strange and old-fashioned, and some of the more fashion-conscious female lawyers have complained that wigs are especially unsuitable for them because they are in a male style. However, many judges say that wearing wigs gives an impression of authority, and that they are a reminder of the long tradition of law in England. Most convincingly, the wearing of wigs makes it harder for criminals to recognise judges outside of court (assuming judges do not wear their wigs then!). According to surveys a majority of British people want judges to continue the practice of wearing wigs.

Judges usually allow lawyers to take wigs off in court in very hot weather. They are no longer worn in family courts in England because they can make children frightened or nervous.

A wig costs around £1,000 - £2,000, and judges receive a clothing allowance to help them pay for wigs and court clothing.

London's oldest tailors and suppliers of judges' wigs

A little further north on Star Yard is a old-style iron toilet shed, now closed.

Return south to Carey St. If you would like to go to Field House to watch an immigration court in action (it is not worth going there just to see the building), **walk east along Carey St, then north on Chancery Lane, then east along Bream's Buildings till you see the court on your left**. The courts are in session Monday to Friday from 9 am to 5 pm except public holidays.

Otherwise, go south down Bell Yard to Fleet St, named after the Fleet River that flows underground here. The expression "Fleet Street" refers to the British newspaper industry, because so many newspapers had offices here. The big national newspapers have all left but a few smaller news organisations remain, and in fact recently a few new ones have moved in.

Turn right on Fleet St and walk west to the main entrance of the Royal Courts of Justice.

Royal Courts of Justice

The Royal Courts of Justice are in a grand Gothic building, opened by Queen Victoria in 1882 and now occupied by the High Court (previously they were in the Houses of Parliament). The building's architect, George Street, probably regretted ever becoming involved. During construction the government insisted on endless minor design changes to cut costs, which

Gothic frontage of the Royal Courts of Justice

reportedly almost drove Street mad. The stress and overwork caused his death the year before the building was completed.

The main gateway where you are standing can frequently be seen on news reports as celebrities or lawyers make speeches to the media on the steps.

Perhaps surprisingly, much of this spectacular building is open to everyone – members of the public can visit the building just for interest, to see the exhibitions and even to sit in a courtroom and watch part of a trial. Your author highly recommends that you watch a trial, because it is an interesting experience that will make a strong impression on you. If you are not sure that you will be welcome, please do not worry. Visitors are so welcome that the building actually produces a free self-guided walk sheet for visitors that takes them around the main points of interest. Judges are used to visitors (mostly young law students) sitting in the visitors' areas of courtrooms, and are probably pleased that you are showing an interest! The courts are open to the public for a very good reason: to show that they operate in a fair way.

Enter the building and pass through the security check. In front of you is an enquiry desk, where you can get a copy of the Royal Courts of Justice's own self-guided walk. In case they have no copies, or in case you would prefer to read the easy English of this book, follow the version below.

You are in the Main Hall, which looks like the hall of a castle; its beautiful mosaic floor was laid by hand. You will probably see lawyers and court staff walking around busily. Behind the Enquiry Desk is a display case marked Daily Case Lists, which lists the trials that are happening that day.

Walk north to the far end of the hall and go through the doors and up some steps into the Crypt Corridor. Ahead and to the left is a café; ahead and to the right are see two pillars with carved decorations. These were made by German workers during a strike by British stonemasons (stone workers). They were sleeping inside the building because it was too dangerous for them to go outside, and

in the evenings they amused themselves by making these carvings, until they were discovered and stopped.

When you turn around to go back into Main Hall you will see one unfinished pillar. The building's architect, George Street, believed that only God could create perfection, so he intentionally left the pillar incomplete so that the building would be imperfect.

Go back into Main Hall. On your left is the entrance to the cells (temporary prison).

Walk south back to the Enquiry Desk. On your left (east of the Enquiry Desk) is a statue of George Street, looking tired and stressed, as he in fact was during construction.

Continue south and then go through a doorway on your left, past a display of judge's robes from Scotland, Italy, Spain, Germany and Luxembourg, all worn by models with ghostly faces. **Go right along the corridor and then up the stairs, following the signs to Courts 1-10. At the top of the stairs one corridor leads straight ahead and another to the right. Many of the building's oldest courtrooms are to be found here, and you are welcome to enter and watch the trials.**

You will be able to see by looking through the windows if a trial is happening; also, there are usually handwritten signs outside the court doors giving details of the trial. If you would like to watch part of a trial, you may like to choose one which seems interesting. Trials involving property law or financial law are extremely technical and may be of less interest. Choose a trial involving a kind of crime you understand!

When you enter a courtroom, open the first door, and you will then see two more doors. The door straight in front of you leads into the main part of the court, and the door to the left or right side leads to the visitors section. When you enter a court it is the custom to bow (lower your head for a moment) slightly to the judge, but probably no one will notice whether you do or not.

The courtrooms, like the building, are mostly late Victorian in design and

Twinings, one of London's oldest shops

private. When you are ready to leave, go back to Main Hall and leave the same way you entered.

As you come out of the Royal Courts of Justice, turn left and walk east. On the south side of the road at no. 216 is Twinings, established in 1706 and one of the oldest shops in London. Most scholars (yes, there is huge argument in the halls of academia about this!) accept that Twinings was the first firm that produced Earl Grey tea.

A little way east of Twinings is a branch of Lloyds Bank with the most amazing decoration you are ever likely to see inside a bank. It was installed for a restaurant in the late nineteenth century, but after the restaurant closed the decoration had of course to be kept.

Temple Bar

A short way further east, where Bell Lane joins Fleet Street, a griffin statue in the centre of the road marks the boundary between the city of "London" and the "City of London". The two are not the same – perhaps it is an attempt to confuse

construction. One wall will be full of legal books. Each judge seems to have a green desk lamp. All the senior participants will be wearing wigs. The atmosphere is of course usually quietly formal, and you will probably not see any dramatic scenes. The lawyers and judges are very serious and intelligent people, and the conversation between them is often interesting to watch, as is the cross-examination, which is when they ask questions of the defendant (the possible criminal) and the witnesses (the people who saw the crime happening).

Even if you do not understand everything that is being said, it is still definitely worth seeing part of a trial even if only for a few minutes.

Near Court 19 (follow the court numbers in order) is the Main Costume Gallery, an exhibition room with a display of various types of judges' robes.

You can explore the whole building except for areas which are specifically

Griffin statue on the site of Temple Bar

tourists. As we mention in other walks, the "City of London", with a capital "C", covers roughly the original site chosen by the Romans to build Londinium. For centuries that area was "London", and "Westminster", where Parliament and Westminster Abbey stand, was a separate city. It was only in the eighteenth century that London began to spread significantly beyond what is now the "City".

Today the "City of London" is still geographically in London but technically not part of London, and has its own separate police force, and its own Lord Mayor, a different person from the Mayor of London. If the Mayor of London comes to the City of London and tries to tell everyone what to do, the Lord Mayor of London can turn up and send him away.

All the main entrances into the City of London had stone gateways, but by 1800 all except one had been knocked down because they were blocking traffic. The last one, Temple Bar, remained on this spot until 1878, when the City of London Corporation took it to pieces and sold it to a wealthy landowner, who rebuilt it on his estate to the north of London. In 2003 the Temple Bar Trust bought it back and rebuilt it near St Paul's Cathedral, where we will see it later in the walk.

A few metres east of the griffin statue, on the south side of the road, is a gateway that leads to Middle Temple and Inner Temple, the last two inns, which are situated side by side. **If the gate is closed, you will need to walk to the alternative gate on Old Mitre Court (see map).** Whichever entrance you use, you can walk around the inns in a circle and leave from the same gate through which you entered.

This walks assumes you enter from the Strand. If you enter from Old Mitre Court, simply go into the inns, follow the circular walk on the map, going clockwise, and leave Temple via the same gate you entered.

Stand in the Strand gateway and look down the hill into the inns.

Middle Temple and Inner Temple
We have explained that the City of London is in London but not part of it. We regret to inform you that that is not the end of

Cobblestones of Middle Temple Lane

the story. The two final inns, Middle Temple and Inner Temple, are in London and in the City of London but not part of either, because of complicated legal arguments 800 years ago which your author was not tempted to research. All we need to know is that if the Mayor of London or the Lord Mayor of the City of London come to these two inns and try to use their authority, the locals can shut the gates in their faces.

Legal arguments over ancient disputes like these provide well-paid work for the people in the pleasant inns where you are standing. Their fine architecture has made them popular with film-makers, and nowadays they are very pleasant places to walk around, work in and live in. It was not always so – Charles Dickens says in his 1830s book Pickwick Papers:

All over the Temple are dark and dirty chambers, the offices of lawyers, where judgements are signed, declarations filed, and numerous other legal machines put in

motion for the torture and misery of ordinary people and for the comfort and benefit of lawyers. Their rooms are usually damp and full of papers hundreds of years old, smelling of rotten wood and cheap candles.
[transliterated into easier English]

Walk south down Middle Temple Lane. When you reach Essex Court and Brick Court, which are really just one court, cross to its west side and walk through the passage to the smaller New Court.
From there walk south into Fountain Court. There has been a fountain here since 1681, and it was mentioned in Charles Dickens' *Martin Chuzzlewit.*
On the south side of Fountain Court is Middle Temple Hall, built around 1574. Inside is a large oak table presented by

Queen Elizabeth I; a smaller table is made from wood from Sir Francis Drake's ship the Golden Hind, one of the first ships to sail around the world.

Peaceful Fountain Court

Amusing English Laws

Legal, royal and religious situations from centuries ago caused the writing of many laws which are still in force today but in modern England seem just a little strange. For example:

- It is illegal to stick a stamp on a letter upside-down if the stamp displays the Queen's head. This is high treason (disloyalty to your country or monarch), and until 1998 the punishment for this in Britain could technically be death
- A pregnant woman can go to the toilet (via either of the two methods) wherever she wants
- Taxi drivers must ask all their passengers if they have smallpox or the plague (fatal diseases)
- A law from 1307 says that if a dead whale is found on an English beach, its head belongs to the king and its tail to the queen, in case the bone was needed for her corset (a piece of clothing that holds the body in the desired shape)
- It is illegal to shake a carpet in a London street
- You may not keep pigs in front of your house

On the other hand, if you are a "freeman of the City of London", you have special (disputed) rights, including the following:

- According to a law of 1189, you may take sheep or cows across London Bridge without paying a fee (this has actually been done several times in recent years)
- You do not have to join the navy
- If you are sentenced to death by hanging, a silk rope must be used.

The good news is that anyone over the age of 21 can apply to become a freeman of the City of London, women included, at a cost of £25. Around 1,800 applications are approved every year.

The sixteenth-century Middle Temple Hall

Inner Temple Gardens

Leave Fountain Court by its south-eastern corner, walk south a few metres then go east along Crown Office Row. On your right are the Inner Temple Gardens, on a lower level than the path. The slope in the land on the north side of the garden was the bank of the River Thames before the Victoria Embankment was built.

North of Crown Office Row, just before you reach the café on the left, is Inner Temple Hall. The original building dated from the eighth century and lasted for around 1,000 years before it had to be replaced in 1870.

At the end of Crown Office Row you enter a large square, Kings Bench Walk. Turn left and walk north up the hill, then turn left and go through an alleyway into Church Court.

On the right is the Master's House, with a well-kept garden.

Just west of that is Temple Church, which has given its name to Temple Bar and the nearby Temple tube station. The church was built in 1185 by the Knights Templar; its round design is based on the Church of the Holy Sepulchre in Jerusalem. It was used as a location in both the book and film versions of *The Da Vinci Code*.

Walk west from Church Court into Hare Court, a quiet and attractive square.

Inner Temple Hall, a rebuilding of the eighth-century original

Kings Bench Walk, often used in films

The Master's House, Inner Temple

Temple Church, seen in **The Da Vinci Code**

Continue east and cross Fetter Lane. On the south side of the road next to a wine shop is a large grey stone building with an archway that leads to Serjeant's Inn, another former inn, recently converted to a hotel.

Not legal-related but worth a few minutes of our time is a short walk through some of the medieval alleyways off Fleet St to see the house of Dr Johnson, creator of the first English dictionary in 1755. Go north up Johnson's Court and enter Gough Square. Johnson's former home, now a museum, is on the square's west side and is open to visitors. A statue of Johnson's cat stands at the eastern end of the square, and underneath it are two of Johnson's many famous quotes. Exit the square via its south-eastern corner into Hind Court, then leave that by its south-eastern corner and walk down Wine Office Court.

Return to Church Court and leave it via its south-western corner, walk west through Pump Court and back into Middle Temple Lane, then walk back north to Fleet St.

Fleet St

Walk east on Fleet St. No. 17 on the south side of the road, with its black-and-white overhanging frontage, is one of very few buildings left today in the City of London that survived the Great Fire of 1666.

A little further east on the north side of the road is St Dunstan's Church, where there are free musical concerts on Wednesday lunchtimes. It is also used by the Romanian Orthodox Church in London. Just west of the church is a small alleyway, at the end of which is a gate marked "Cliffords Inn", marking the site of another former inn.

Just east of St Dunstan's at no. 14 the names of several newspapers can be seen on the building's front and sides, a reminder of Fleet St's newspaper past.

One of the few pre-Fire buildings that survive in London

On your left near the end of Wine Office Court is Ye Olde Cheshire Cheese, built in 1667 and famous for its many original features. Its lack of natural lighting and real coal fire create a strange but still homely atmosphere. Samuel Johnson and Dickens are known to have eaten and drunk here, as are several other literary figures.

Back on Fleet St, continue east. At no. 66 on the south side of the road is The Tipperary, a pub whose sign outside claims that the River Fleet runs underneath it. This is incorrect – The Fleet runs north to south along the bottom of the valley ahead – but unfortunately the sign's claim has been repeated by many authors since.

Continue east across Farringdon St, where the Fleet really does flow under the road towards the Thames, and continue up the hill in the direction of St Paul's Cathedral. When you reach Old Bailey, turn left and walk north to the main

The seventeenth-century "Cheshire Cheese" pub and restaurant, unique and atmospheric

entrance of the Central Criminal Court on your right.

Old Bailey

To most people in Britain "Old Bailey" means the Central Criminal Court, but it is in fact the street on which the court stands. It really is lucky that your author is here to correct everyone else's mistakes.

From 1188 there were prisons on this site, most recently the terrible Newgate Prison. Until 1868 public hangings were held in the street where you are standing. Bloodthirsty crowds would gather to watch the show, and throw rubbish and stones at the prisoner. A tunnel was dug from the church you see just north of here to the prison so that a priest could attend to the prisoner without having to force his way through the angry gathering. It is not the first prison tunnel ever dug, but perhaps the first one dug by the prison managers.

St Dunstan's Church, and reminders of Fleet Street's newspaper past

The Central Criminal Court, venue for Britain's most important trials

At that time the Old Bailey was a small court attached to the prison, but in 1902 the prison was demolished and the present court building constructed. The famous bronze statue on top of the building's dome is Lady Justice, with a

sword in one hand and the scales of justice in the other, representing the careful weighing (balancing) of evidence for and evidence against.

Some of the most infamous people in British history have been convicted at the Old Bailey, including the poisoner Dr Crippen, the Kray twins, the Yorkshire Ripper, and Ruth Ellis, the last woman to be hanged in Britain.

If the building is open you are welcome to enter the building and watch trials in progress – if you are sure they will let you out again.

Continue north up Old Bailey, turn right on Newgate St then right again into Warwick Lane. Walk south then turn west into Paternoster Square, recently smartened up and home to the London Stock Exchange at no. 10. **On the southern side of the square is Temple Bar, the gate that formerly stood on The Strand. Walk south through the gate to St Paul's Cathedral.**

The scales of justice on the "Old Bailey"

Temple Bar on its new site in Paternoster Square

St Paul's Cathedral

The iconic St Paul's Cathedral is so well covered by other literature that we will mention it only briefly here. The cathedral is Sir Christopher Wren's greatest work, constructed to replace St Paul's Church which was destroyed in the Great Fire of London in 1666. Before that there were Saxon churches on the site, and possibly a Roman temple even earlier.

St Paul's is one of the earliest Baroque buildings in England. It has witnessed some notable events in British history including the funerals of Lord Nelson, the Duke of Wellington and Winston Churchill; the marriage of Prince Charles and Lady Diana Spencer; and the present queen's eightieth birthday celebrations.

Small children often recognise St Paul's Cathedral from the film *Mary Poppins*; the song Feed the Birds features an old lady selling birdseed at "tuppence a bag" on the cathedral steps. On a recent visit, your author's children were disappointed not to see her here.

To see St Paul's – or rather a small model of it – in the film, search on YouTube for "Feed The Birds - Mary Poppins (Julie Andrews)".

Walk anti-clockwise around the cathedral to admire its view from all sides. The walk ends at St Paul's tube station, just north-east of the cathedral.

St Paul's Cathedral, as viewed from Ludgate Hill

Government London

Start:	Charing Cross tube station
End:	St James's Park tube station
Length:	2.5 miles (4 kilometres)
Time taken:	1.5 hours
Eat and drink:	There are a few restaurants around Charing Cross station including the Sherlock Holmes, which provides pub meals. The Grosvenor Café at 60 Horseferry Rd makes delicious sandwiches using fresh-roasted meat. There are many restaurants on Strutton Ground and in the streets at its western end
Includes:	Sherlock Holmes pub, Great Scotland Yard, Whitehall, the Ministry of Defence, 10 Downing St, the Houses of Parliament, the Jewel Tower (built in 1366 to house royal jewels), Victoria Tower Gardens, Millbank, Westminster School, Strutton Ground Market, New Scotland Yard
Best time:	Any. The area is more peaceful on a Sunday, but it has more atmosphere on weekdays, when Whitehall is full of civil servants and politicians. If you want to visit the Jewel Tower, check its irregular opening times by Googling "jewel tower English heritage". You could also do the walk after dark, when the Houses of Parliament are lit up and the River Thames is at its most atmospheric

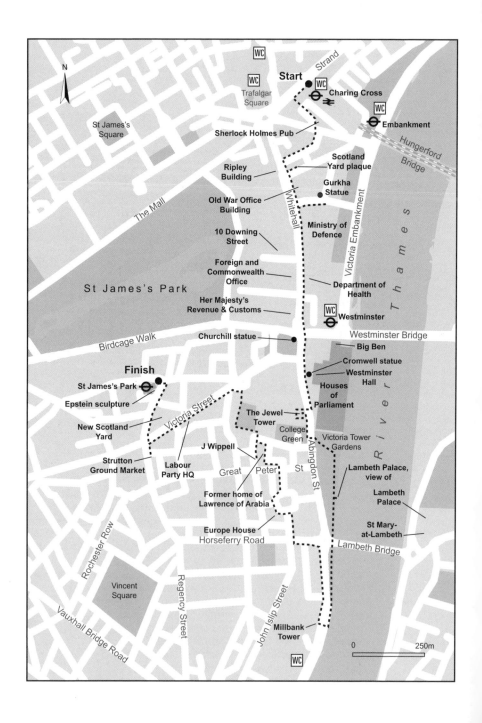

Introduction

This book includes both a Royal London walk and a Government London walk. A few hundred years ago those two walks would have been just one, because royalty and government were the same thing.

Today, who governs Britain? According to some, Britain is not governed from London at all because most of the really important decisions are made either by the European Parliament or by business leaders in financial centres like New York, Tokyo and Singapore. However, when things go wrong plenty of people in Britain blame the government for almost everything, so presumably they think it has at least some power.

This walk takes you to some of the main sites in London's political heartland. Have no fear, we will not be discussing politics or the workings of government. The walk focuses instead on some magnificent buildings, quiet historic streets and squares, and it even includes a James Bond film location.

On a working day you will probably see many civil servants (officials working in government ministries and departments) in the area, especially if you are there at around 4 pm, when – some say – they leave for home! If you know your British politicians, you may recognise some famous faces in the streets around Parliament.

Walk

Leave Charing Cross tube station by exit number 5 and walk west, stopping at the corner of Strand and Northumberland St. From there, look west to Trafalgar Square where you will see the towering structure of Nelson's Column. Many of London's politically correct schoolchildren think the statue on the top is of Nelson Mandela, but in fact Horatio Nelson was a naval captain who was killed during the Battle of Trafalgar in 1805. The square is a popular place for political meetings and New Year's Eve celebrations.

Turn left into Northumberland St and walk south towards Northumberland Avenue. Just before you reach the avenue is the Sherlock Holmes pub, with an interesting replica of the famous detective's room inside on the first floor (if "replica" is the correct word for something that was always fictional in any case) and photographs of the many famous actors who have played Sherlock Holmes. You can go in and see the displays without being a customer.

Opposite the pub is the Korean Cultural Centre on the corner, which usually has free exhibitions you can visit. **Cross to the south side of Northumberland Avenue and walk east a few metres past the Nigerian Cultural Centre, then stand on the corner of Northumberland Avenue and Great Scotland Yard.**

Great Scotland Yard

Walk to no. 13-15 Great Scotland Yard on your right, which is the Civil Service Club, a gentleman's club for civil servants. Regular comedy nights are held here; apparently it is important for civil servants, who work all day with the

The Civil Service Club, Great Scotland Yard

government, to have a good sense of humour.

"Scotland Yard" is of course an internationally famous expression for the detective branch of London's Metropolitan Police, whose headquarters were here before they moved in the 1960s. Today there exists here just one reminder of the street's glorious crimefighting days. Walk a short way west to no. 7 Great Scotland Yard, which is the stables of the horses of the Metropolitan Police Mounted Branch. No number is visible but you can see a stone carving of two horses high up on the building's front.

Stables of the Metropolitan Police, the only remaining police connection with Great Scotland Yard

Stand at the entrance and you will probably be able to smell the horses but not see them. Just inside the building's archway is a board on which is written the current number of horses in the building, so that if fire breaks out the fire brigade know how many horses are to be rescued. Very sensible, no doubt, but it does mean that when a police officer needs to rush out of the building on horseback to catch a murderer he must first mentally subtract one from that number, get off his horse, rub out the existing number, write the new one and get back on his horse before he can ride off, which must be annoying.

A little further west at no. 1, set back from the street, is a Victorian town house where there was once a police museum displaying weapons used in murders and assaults in London. The museum still

1 Great Scotland Yard, formerly a police museum

exists in the Metropolitan Police's new building but is not open to the public.

At the western end of the street is The Clarence, a pub associated with civil

The Clarence pub, popular with civil servants

Scottish Law in London?

According to a New York Times article of 1964, Great Scotland Yard is so called because it was the site of the Scottish Embassy in England so was therefore legally part of Scotland. The two countries were joined together by the Treaty of Union in 1707 but their legal systems were not, and remain separate to this day. This means, some say, that Scottish law may technically still be in force in the street where you are standing. Therefore, we warn you to be aware of some of the differences between Scottish and English law while in this street:

- While in Great Scotland Yard, Scottish law allows you to marry when you reach the age of 16. In the surrounding streets you must wait until you are 18, or get your parents' permission

- If you build a house in Great Scotland Yard, according to Scottish law the windows in the upper floors need to be washable from inside the house, for safety reasons. In any other London street, English law generously allows you to risk your life by washing your windows in whatever dangerous manner you choose

- If you drive through the streets of London smoking a cigarette in a company car, you will be treated as a respectable lady or gentleman. As soon as you turn the corner into Great Scotland Yard, however, you are breaking the law, and any Scottish policeman who sees your crime will immediately arrest you.

It has been joked many times that the quickest way to understand the differences between Scottish and English law is to commit the same crime in both countries and see what happens.

---

servants, hence the gentlemanly-looking bowler hat on the sign.

Stand by The Clarence and look across to the Ripley Building on the west side of Whitehall (there is no need to cross the road).

Whitehall

On the western side of Whitehall is the Ripley Building, built in 1726 as the first office building in Britain. It is used by the Cabinet Office, a government department which provides support to the Prime Minister and the cabinet (government ministers). The front view of the building is greatly spoilt by the stone screen which was added in 1788.

Walk south then turn left into Whitehall Place and walk east 50 metres to the main entrance of the Department for

Ripley Building, Britain's first purpose-built office building

Energy and Climate Change (what some countries call "ministries" are usually called "departments" in Britain). A blue plaque to the left of the building's

Plaque marking the first site of Britain's most famous police department

doorway marks the original site of Scotland Yard.

Return to Whitehall and walk south. The enormous building on your left is The Old War Office, formerly the administrative centre of the British Army and now used by the Ministry of Defence.

Entrance to the Old War Office building

You may be able to enter the foyer and look around.

Continue south down Whitehall and turn left into Horse Guards Avenue. On your left is a side entrance to the Old War Office, with a view into its yard. Over the archways are symbols for Wales, England and Ireland: a dragon, three lions, and a harp.

Further east along Horse Guards Avenue is a statue of a Gurkha, commissioned in 1997. The Gurkhas have been a brigade in the British Army since 1817.

Gurkha statue in Horse Guards Avenue

On the south side of the road is the impressive entrance to the Ministry of Defence, one of only two government departments with "ministry" in their name (the other being the Ministry of Justice). The two stone figures over the doorway represent Earth and Water.

It is not illegal to photograph the Ministry of Defence, but if you do you may be asked to explain yourself. When your author photographed the building's entrance the ministry police stopped him and did a polite security check on him,

1930s frontage of the Ministry of Defence

Downing St

10 Downing Street has been the official London residence of the Prime Minister since 1735.

Until 1982 anyone could walk up to 10 Downing Street and photograph the Prime Minister's house. The black gates you now see were installed to prevent this, and security checks are made on anyone trying to enter the street. Your author decided not to – two security checks in one day would have made even he himself believe he was a criminal.

During the Second World War the then Prime Minister Winston Churchill usually slept in an underground bunker for safety but he made sure he was often photographed entering and leaving 10 even after being humorously warned that the event would be reported in full in this book.

Under the Ministry of Defence building are the wine cellars from the original Whitehall Palace, which was built by Henry VIII on this site and mostly destroyed by fire in 1698 (see the Royal London walk). The cellars survived underground and have been preserved to this day. When the present ministry building was constructed the cellars had to be carefully moved three metres to the west and six metres deeper.

The streets of Whitehall cover so many historical remains that great care has to be taken not to damage it when doing any building or excavation work. If you notice any building work taking place during your walk, you will probably see on the site an official whose jacket bears the words Pre Construct Archaeology. It is his or her job to watch over construction projects and make sure no archaeological remains are destroyed, even if this means temporarily stopping the building work.

Return to Whitehall and walk south, passing on your left the Wales Office with its sign in English and Welsh. On the opposite side of Whitehall the building with the four-pillared portico is the Scottish Office.

When you reach the traffic lights, cross Whitehall to Downing Street.

Rats in Downing Street

On guard inside 10 Downing Street is the "Chief Mouser", a cat whose duty is to kill the rats in the Prime Minister's house (your author has never had an easier opportunity to make a joke). The tradition of an official governmental mouser dates back to the sixteenth century.

Until January 2011 the job of Chief Mouser was unfilled, but after rats were seen running through Downing St in the background of a news report, a decision was instantly taken at the highest levels of government to deal with the crisis. Prime Minister David Cameron and his family recruited a feline civil servant, named him Larry and apparently gave orders to kill on sight.

Soon after his arrival in Downing St Larry scratched a female news reporter's arm, so perhaps he misunderstood his instructions – or perhaps not. At any rate, he caught no mice or rats during his first two months in Downing St, and there have been many calls for his resignation.

To see the rat running along Downing St and Larry's vicious attack on the female news reporter, Google "Don't mess with me Downing Street ratcatcher", open the first result and scroll down.

View of 10 Downing Street

Downing St to give the impression that all was normal.

Back on Whitehall

Cross back to the east side of Whitehall and continue south. When you reach the Department of Health on your left, look to the west side of Whitehall. The nearest of

Remembrance Day wreaths at the Cenotaph in Whitehall

the two huge white stone buildings is the Foreign and Commonwealth Office, with stone carvings on its walls representing the world's continents; south of that, and much less popular, is Her Majesty's Revenue and Customs, which collects taxes. Unfortunately it is one of the most effective departments of government.

The memorial in the middle of Whitehall is the Cenotaph, where a service is held in November every year to remember soldiers killed in war. In more respectful times, most men who walked past it would raise their hats.

Continue south. On the corner of Whitehall and Bridge St is the Parliamentary Bookshop, which sells government-related publications.

Houses of Parliament

The Houses of Parliament, seen from Whitehall

At the southern end of Whitehall are, of course, the Houses of Parliament, address of the British government and one of the most recognisable buildings in the world. The clock tower at the north end is informally called Big Ben and can be seen in almost every film set in London, usually with a red bus or black taxi driving past it.

Walk south along St Margaret St past Parliament Square on your right, where a statue of Winston Churchill in the north-east corner watches the mad traffic nightmare with displeasure. There are usually protesters in the square, with their banners facing towards Parliament.

Continue south until you are level with Westminster Hall, the oldest part of the Houses of Parliament. It was built in

Westminster Hall, the oldest part of the Parliament complex, built around 1097

1097 and is one of only two surviving sections of the previous Palace of Westminster, which was mostly destroyed by fire in 1834, after which the present Houses of Parliament were constructed. It is supposed to be a great honour for a foreign leader to be allowed to make a speech to Parliament in Westminster Hall. The lucky few include Pope Benedict XVI, Nelson Mandela and Barack Obama.

On the western side of Westminster Hall is a statue of Oliver Cromwell, the seventeenth-century politician and military leader who brought down the

Statue of republican Oliver Cromwell

monarchy and put in place a republican government, which lasted eleven years until the monarchy was restored. For four years after his death his head was displayed on a pole where his statue now stands.

The long black wooden structure in the road in front of the Houses of Parliament is a blast barrier to prevent car bombs from damaging the buildings.

Walk to the southern end of the Houses of Parliament and cross St Margaret's St to Old Palace Yard, a street name with an obvious origin. Russian visitors to London could be forgiven for thinking the white statue in the yard is of Tsar Nicholas II, but it is in fact King George V, Nicholas's cousin; the two looked very much alike.

Immediately north-west of Old Palace Yard you can see the back of Westminster Abbey.

Old Palace Yard was where Guy Fawkes met his end. He was a seventeenth-century Catholic who planned to destroy the entire Protestant government by blowing up (exploding) the Palace of Westminster while King James I and his ministers were inside, so that a Catholic monarchy could be restored. His plan was discovered, and he was brought to Old Palace Yard to be hanged, but he jumped from the platform to his death before the hanging could take place.

Since then, November 5th of each year has been known in Britain as Bonfire Night or Guy Fawkes Night. Firework displays are held, and a dressed-up model of Guy Fawkes, known as the "guy", is burnt on a bonfire (leading many people to think, incorrectly, that Guy Fawkes was burnt alive as a punishment).

The word "guy" came to mean any strangely-dressed person, but in America it later simply referred to a man, a meaning which has of course become common today.

The Jewel Tower

Go to the south-western corner of the yard and walk south to the Jewel Tower, another part of the Palace of Westminster which survived the 1834 fire. It was built in 1366 to house King Edward III's private

The fourteenth-century Jewel Tower

treasure. Inside is an exhibition called *Parliament Past and Present*.

Go back onto the main road and walk south a short way to College Green, a small park with a Henry Moore sculpture. You can often see TV journalists interviewing politicians here because they can be filmed with the Houses of Parliament in the background.

Victoria Tower Gardens

Cross to the east side of Abingdon Road and enter Victoria Tower Gardens at its northernmost gate. The statue by the entrance is of Emmeline Pankhurst, a militant campaigner for women's right to vote. A little further ahead is a

reproduction of French sculptor Rodin's *The Burghers of Calais*. South of that is the Buxton Memorial, designed in 1865 as a memorial to the end of slavery in the British Empire.

Now walk to the eastern side of the park for a view across the river to Lambeth Palace, official residence of the Archbishop of Canterbury, leader of the Church of England. The church tower a little way south of the palace is St Mary-at-Lambeth, where Captain Bligh of the Bounty mutiny is buried. The story has been filmed many times. To see five minutes of the most dramatic bits from the 1984 version starring Anthony Hopkins and Mel Gibson, search on YouTube for "The Bounty (1984) - William Bligh Highlights".

Leave the park at its southern end, cross the road and continue south by the riverside through Victoria Gardens South, at the southern end of which you will see Millbank Tower.

Millbank Tower

Millbank Tower is a modern office complex where the Conservative Party has its headquarters, as do several other governmental organisations. It is built on the site of a former prison where prisoners were held before being transported to Australia in the nineteenth century.

From the street outside Millbank Tower, to the south-east across the river you can see

Lambeth Palace, home of the Archbishop of Canterbury

Thorney Island

Until the nineteenth century, the River Tyburn could be seen flowing south above ground in Westminster, dividing into two just before it reached the Thames and creating Thorney Island (see picture). The island's land was less marshy (wet) than nearby areas, the Thames was easy to cross here, and the island had a hill that could be used as a lookout point; all reasons why the Romans built a small town on this site. The first church here may have been built in around 604.

The island was thought of as a holy place, which is why in 1050 King Edward the Confessor began to build Westminster Abbey here. At that time English kings did not live in a fixed place – they moved around a great deal; but when the construction of Westminster Abbey began, Edward built the Palace of Westminster nearby so he could live there and watch over the building work. The fact that Edward lived on this site

Former shape of Thorney Island, showing Parliament and Westminster Abbey for orientation (image reproduced by kind permission of Andy Chopping, Museum of London Archaeology)

permanently meant that Westminster became the capital of England. "London" was a completely separate city, about two miles away and not a royal centre but a business area.

Travel by land was difficult and uncomfortable in those days, but from Westminster Edward and later monarchs could easily move by river, which is why many of England's other palaces were built beside the Thames, for example Richmond, Hampton Court, Greenwich and Windsor.

The tradition of a royal barge (boat) dates back to 1215. At present, although there are 24 official Royal Watermen receiving a salary of £3.50 a year, there is no official royal barge, but plans to build one were released in December 2012 to mark the sixtieth anniversary of the Queen's coronation. To see a one-minute BBC news report of the design, Google "Queen's Diamond Jubilee royal barge design unveiled".

Over time, of course, London and Westminster have grown into one city called London, but the area where you are now standing is after nearly 1,000 years still the royal, governmental and religious centre of the city, and the original area that was London is still the business centre (with the entertainment centre of London lying between the two – see the Theatre London walk).

There is no visible sign of Thorney Island today. The Tyburn River now flows underground, the marshes were built over, and engineer Joseph Bazalgette built the Thames Embankment which is under your feet.

The picture shows the present-day Houses of Parliament and Westminster Abbey on the actual site of Thorney Island as it used to look.

Millbank Tower, with many political associations

the dramatic architecture of 85 Vauxhall Cross, home of the government's foreign intelligence service MI6. The building has appeared in three James Bond films, most memorably *The World Is Not Enough*, when James Bond crashes out of an upper floor window in a speedboat and chases a suspect's yacht down the River Thames, somehow always with London's most photogenic sights in the background. To

see the excitement, search on YouTube for "The World Is Not Enough - River Thames Boat Chase (Rescore)". 85 Vauxhall Cross is only visible briefly at the start.

Westminster Abbey Environs

Return north to the roundabout. Centuries ago, when the Thames was wider and the water level lower, a horse-drawn ferry owned by the Archbishop of Canterbury regularly crossed the river here until a bridge was built in 1862 (not the current one, which dates from 1932). Most of London's bridges are built on the site of old ferry crossings, which were often manned just by a single boatman and a rowing-boat. Four ancient ferry services still cross the Thames outside central London, though all are now motorised – the last rowing-boat service ended in the 1920s.

Go west into Horseferry Rd, turn right into Dean Bradley St then continue north into Smith Square, a peaceful spot where many governmental organisations are based.

Walk to the south-west corner of the square where you will see Europe House, formerly the Conservative Party headquarters and now the London base of the European Parliament and the European Commission. If the building is open you may see a portrait of European Commission President José Manuel Barroso on the wall inside.

Walk to the north side of the square and leave it via Lord North St, which has been home to numerous famous political

85 Vauxhall Cross, home of MI6

Europe House, London base of the European Parliament and the European Commission

figures including former prime minister Harold Wilson, then continue across Great Peter St into Cowley St, then go left into Barton Street and follow it round to the right. At no. 14 a blue plaque marks the former home of TE Lawrence, nicknamed Lawrence of Arabia.

From here you will feel the presence of Westminster Abbey close by, as many church-related organisations are clustered in the area.

At the end of Barton St turn left then left again into Tufton St. At no. 11 is an interesting and ancient-looking shop which – you never know – you might need one day: J Wippell and Company Ltd, suppliers of clothing to bishops, priest and other church officials.

Westminster schoolboys

Suppliers of church clothing

Go back north up Tufton St and through the small alleyway into Dean's Yard, part of Westminster Abbey, whose roof you can see ahead. In the south-eastern corner of the yard is Westminster School, one of the most famous private schools in Britain, and also one of the oldest, dating back to around 1179. Former pupils include Christopher Wren, architect of St Paul's Cathedral; AA Milne, author of the Winnie-the-Pooh books; Andrew Lloyd Webber, composer of musicals including *Jesus Christ Superstar* and *Evita*; Helena Bonham Carter, star of films such as *Room With A View* and *Planet of the Apes*; Louis Theroux, documentary-maker; and Nick Clegg, current leader of the Liberal Democrats and Deputy Prime Minister. You may be surprised to learn that Shane McGowan, lead singer of the Pogues with a reputation for wild drunkenness, also

attended the school for six months before being asked to leave for drug-taking. Depending when you do this walk, you may see the nation's future leaders walking around in their school uniforms, preparing for the greatness that awaits them.

Go clockwise around the yard, passing Westminster Abbey Choir School on your left (you can see their dining-room through the basement windows), and leave via the north-west corner.

Victoria

Emerge into Victoria St and walk west. On your left are various government departments and offices. On the road's north side after no. 20 you will see Dean Farrar St. You may have noticed that many street names in this area begin with "Dean". A dean is a position of authority in the Church of England, and the nearby Westminster Abbey is led by a dean. Dean

Farrar St is named after Frederick W. Farrar, who in Victorian times would have needed no introduction. He wrote "Eric, or Little by Little", one of the three most popular boys' books of the nineteenth century. "Eric" is a well-meaning schoolboy who "little by little" is pulled into immorality, though his sins – smoking, drinking, petty theft, cheating – perhaps do not seem so very terrible nowadays. The book's moralistic tone would be considered hilarious (very funny) today – even its most recent publishers called it "preposterous" (ridiculous) – but in its time it was highly influential.

Continue west along Victoria St. At no. 39 on your left is an uninspiring office building in which the Labour Party has its headquarters. Continue west to the crossroads.

If time allows, Strutton Ground on the left has some attractive shops and a street market on weekdays. Otherwise turn right into Broadway.

Headquarters of the Metropolitan Police

and eastern facades, just above shop height, for a pair of sculptures by Jacob Epstein. When first revealed in 1929 their nudity caused a nationwide scandal. Today, at the risk of a poor pun, they are barely noticed.

Market in Strutton Ground

A short way up the street is New Scotland Yard on your right with its famous turning sign, representing the police's continual watching of the city all around them. At least, that is what your author thinks it might represent. Perhaps it is just a sign that turns round for no reason.

Continue north past the Falklands Government Offices to 55 Broadway, the gigantic headquarters of London Underground, where the walk ends.

Before you enter St James's Park tube station, look on the building's northern

55 Broadway, headquarters of London Underground

Also from Sigma Leisure:

London Guide in Easy English

compiled by Patrick Gubbins

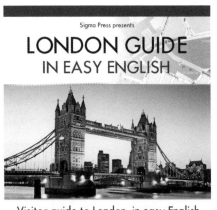

Sigma Press presents

LONDON GUIDE IN EASY ENGLISH

Visitor guide to London, in easy English
- Sights
- Restaurants
- Art, culture, sport
- Night life
- Hotels
- and more!

Millions of visitors come to London every year on holiday, and guess what? They don't all speak perfect English! London Guide in Easy English helps them enjoy their stay by explaining the city in clear, simple language that even basic speakers can understand.

The guide covers all the capital's major and minor attractions, hotels, restaurants, parks and green areas and sporting venues, and contains a full directory of necessary information for visitors to London, including advice on working in the city. One of the book's themes is the amazing variety of activities on offer in London, some covered by no other guide, such as whitewater rafting, craft workshops, ski-ing on real snow, visits to courtrooms to watch real trials, and even how to see members of the Royal Family!

Packed with exciting ideas and stunning photography, London Guide in Easy English is the ideal travel companion for the many visitors to London looking for a guide book written at an easy level of English.

ISBN 978-1-85058-937-2
£9.99
Available June 2012

The Charlie Chaplin Walk
Stephen P Smith

The Charlie Chaplin Walk is targeted at fans of Chaplin, those interested in film history, people with a connection to the Lambeth and Kennington areas of London and anybody with an interest of the social history of London's poor of the late Victorian and early Edwardian era.

Explore the London streets of Charlie Chaplin's childhood in a chronological tour that can be taken on foot or from the comfort of an armchair. This book concentrates on the story of Chaplin's formative years and takes a fresh look at the influence they had upon his films.

About the Author:
Stephen Smith has been interested in Charlie Chaplin since reading his obituary in his parent's newspaper, when he was 12. He was surprised to learn that he was English. He became fascinated by his early life and tried to piece together the significant places of his childhood.

ISBN 978-1-85058-852-8
£9.99

Chilling Tales of Old London

Keith Johnson

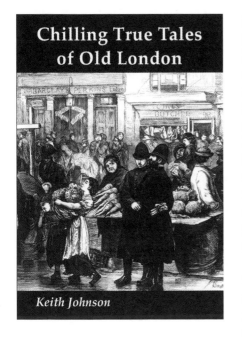

Lock all your doors, draw closer to the fire and let Keith Johnson lead you into the bleakest aspects of London's past. In Chilling True Tales of Old London Keith gives the human stories behind the I 9th Century headlines, giving a fascinating insight into London's past when villainy and vice abounded. Amid the reeking pestilence of a crowded city the poor and prosperous alike live through the toil and torment.

News relayed to the nation often shocked those in the provincial towns as mischief and mayhem all too frequently prevailed. Besides the catastrophes and calamities of everyday life the headlines reported acts of notoriety. No one was safe from the evil doer, be they royalty or ruffian.

In consequence trauma and tribulation were part of life's rich tapestry at the heart of England's empire where the pilferer, poisoner, rogue, rioter, murderer and mischief maker roamed the streets and the alleyways.

About the Author:
Keith Johnson was born in Preston, Lancashire. He is a member of the Crime Writers Association.

ISBN 978-1-85058-871-7
£9.99

All of our books are all available on-line at **www.sigmapress.co.uk** or through booksellers. For a free catalogue, please contact:

Sigma Leisure, Stobart House, Pontyclerc, Penybanc Road, Ammanford, Carmarthenshire SA18 3HP
Tel: 01269 593100   Fax: 01269 596116

info@sigmapress.co.uk   www.sigmapress.co.uk